Faith Can Change
Your World

by

Dr. Lester Sumrall

Faith Can Change Your World

by

Dr. Lester Sumrall

South Bend, Indiana
www.leseapublishing.com

Faith Can Change Your World
ISBN 1-58568-199-7
(This book is a compilation of *Faith Can Change Your World,* formerly registered as ISBN 0-937580-17-1, and *Take It...It's Yours,* formerly registered as ISBN 0-88368-253-2.)

LeSEA Publishing
530 E. Ireland Rd.
South Bend, IN 46614

Contents

Introduction

Faith—believing and speaking God's Word and respecting it as the highest standard of truth—has been called the eye that sees the invisible, the ear that hears the inaudible, the hand that feels the intangible, and the power that works the impossible.

Faith comes, not by prayer, but by continually feeding upon the spiritual food of God's Word (Romans 10:17).

Every human on earth has a capacity for world-changing faith built into his spirit, soul, and body. No one is excluded. Anyone who will accept it can have a relationship with God the Father, with Jesus Christ the Son, and with the Holy Spirit that will change his world.

In this book, *Faith Can Change Your World,* I am trying to get you to believe that God has selected you, just as He did Abraham, to receive unlimited blessings from heaven, and then to show you "how" to possess them. It has been said that no one has beheld the fullness of what God can bring to pass through the fulfillment of faith.

As you study the principles of faith taught in this book and apply them to your life, you will be enabled to raise the standard of God's Word, which will bring change in your life and in the lives of others, both spiritually and naturally.

Now, go, raise the standard of the Word, and make a difference in all the earth!

Endorsements

Dr. Lester Sumrall was a good, personal friend of mine. The times I spent with him were some of the most powerful experiences of my faith life. His boldness in God was as thrilling to me as it was terrifying to the devil.

I asked him one time how he stayed so full of energy and strength. The man went night and day delivering, ministering, laying hands on the sick, etc., almost nonstop. He said with that brightness in his eye and Holy Ghost power in his voice, "I am intensely interested in what I am doing!" At that time he was in his mid-70s and going strong.

The Apostle Paul wrote to Timothy and said, *...faith words nourish....* We need to set our faith on books like this. Our boldness in God must be nourished. Reading and studying the lives of God's boldest warriors like Lester Sumrall encourage our own lives of faith and will bring that same boldness alive in us.

Kenneth Copeland
Kenneth Copeland Ministries
Fort Worth, TX

Dr. Sumrall inspired me in many ways by his preaching and his life. His heart for the people of the world has touched me the most. I still think in amazement of his first trip around the world with Howard Carter. I enjoyed him telling that story time and again. He understood hearing God's voice and obeying by faith.

The blessing today is that we have Dr. Sumrall's writings and recordings available to us. The things he learned, he preached and wrote. The same faith he had can be developed in our lives by hearing and obeying God's voice.

Billy Joe Daugherty
Pastor of Victory Christian Center
Tulsa, OK

The walk of faith is an eternal quest for every believer. And for my friend, the late Dr. Lester Sumrall, it was a way of life. His love for God and vision to change the world became a reality as he dared to trust God for the impossible. His impact upon the world is still being felt. The principles of faith which he learned and applied in over 60 years of ministry are contained in this book. . . principles that can change your life. Discover a new dimension in faith that can help you change your world. You can make a difference.

Benny Hinn
Benny Hinn Ministries
Irving, TX

The first time Lester Sumrall, my mentoring pastor, came to my church the crowd was large, the building too small, and with no other alternative but to display his product outside, I stood helpless as the wind carried it away! Nervously over dinner, in a desperate attempt to redeem myself, I said, "I just need to get more faith." As his baby blue eyes pierced into mine he made a sound I soon learned to identify and asked, "Would you like me to tell you what faith is?" "Yes sir," I responded, leaning so far over the table that my tie fell in my plate. And with that soft, gruff voice I came to cherish, he uttered these words that have been the foundation of my entire life and ministry: "Faith is simply knowing God!"

As you open these pages, Dr. Sumrall's revelation of faith is sure to change your world!

Rod Parsley
Pastor of World Harvest Church
Columbus, OH

Foreword

Very few people have earned the title "worldchanger." Lester Sumrall was one of those few. As a result of his aggressive, take-God-at-His-Word walk of faith, gospel seeds were planted in many nations of the world, when missionary work was very difficult and not too popular.

Although every believer has received a measure of faith, faith is something that grows. It increases by hearing the Word and by putting it to work. Faith needs to be encouraged.

For these reasons, *Faith Can Change Your World* is a vitally important book in the critical time in which we live. Christians who have allowed their faith to become dormant should read this book and be encouraged to do mighty exploits for the Lord's Kingdom.

This book is not only a good exhortation, but there are valuable faith principles to be learned and practiced so the believer can do the things Christ ordained. After all, we did not choose Him, but He chose us and set us apart to bear much fruit (John 15:16).

With very little money, no formal education, and no well-known name, Lester Sumrall was able to plant churches, found television and radio networks, and preach in every corner of the earth. His one great resource was his raw faith in a Risen Lord.

We have much to learn from this man who made it work. Read *Faith Can Change Your World.* Consume it. Digest it. Let it become part of your spiritual mettle. Then go forward and change the world around you.

R. W. Schambach
Schambach Revivals
Tyler, TX

Part I

The Attributes of Faith

1
Faith Can Change Your World

Faith Can Change Your World!

That's a little audacious, wouldn't you say? Faith not just to bless your chickens in the backyard. Faith not just to help your car run. But faith to change the world!

There is a potential in faith that can change the world. The world is changeable. It needs changing. And you're the one to do it!

It is possible that no one ever has released the total power available to him through faith. And that's saying something. Perhaps nobody ever has been totally dedicated to this use of faith—grappling with faith, struggling with faith, until they understand it and know it and reach out to change the world in which we live. You might be that one.

The Power of Faith

Natural man through natural science can explode atomic bombs, releasing megatons of destructive energy. He calls that power—possibly, as far as he knows, power at its ultimate.

But faith like Elijah had when he sealed the heavens from moisture for three years is more powerful than atomic energy. Faith like Elijah had when he prayed and ended the drought with instant and abundant rain demonstrated power beyond natural man's ability to control or even analyze.

Man can push a button and operate mighty machinery. But Moses through faith, with a lift of his hand and the speaking of a word, caused the Red Sea to open. The waters stood up and congealed on either side, the seabed dried, and more than two million people with their herds and flocks walked through without sinking knee-deep in mud. That's the operation of faith!

Faith remains to this day the greatest source of energy available to mankind. Christians today need to learn how to release the phenomenal energy created within us by the thing we call faith. For God does not release His energy without our exercising faith.

Every human on earth has a capacity for world-changing faith built into his tripartite structure (spirit, soul, and body). No one is excluded. Anyone who will accept it can have a relationship with God that can change his world. God gives to everyone who will receive Him the measure of faith (Romans 12:3). This faith releases the blessings of God.

Yet people sometimes think like this: *So-and-so should be blessed. He's gone to church for twenty years.*

God's blessings don't come because someone attended church twenty years. They come when you release something inside you that is a living, dynamic power and force and strength. That something is faith.

In this book we will deal with faith so strongly until you can say: "My faith is strengthened. My faith is heightened. My faith is made a living source of strength in God."

Decide Now to Take These Steps
Toward Faith to Change Your World

1. Know what faith is

God is not ignorant. He cannot condone ignorance. God is intelligence. He wants us to know. He wants us to seek out and find truth. If we go our own way and don't do it, we ostracize ourselves from the mightiness of God and the glories of the Almighty.

God's Word says, *My people are destroyed for lack of knowledge* (Hosea 4:6). The Hebrew word translated *destroyed* means "cut off." God's people are cut off from His blessings for lack of knowledge.

In any land where there is ignorance of God and His blessings, there is trouble. God cannot bless unbelief. Unbelief exists where people do not have sufficient knowledge. Knowledge brings release from ignorance. Knowledge helps people know what they can receive from God.

It is up to us to learn how to release our faith, to learn how to move with God, to learn how to say: "Lord, I know You can and will do it. I'm as good as Abraham, Moses, or anyone else. I'm a child of the King, and I'm going to release the mighty power available to me through faith."

2. Accept what God says as Absolute Truth

If you cannot accept what God says as truth, you cannot enter the realm of faith. When you walk in the faith realm, you remove yourself from this world—what the eyes see, the ears hear, the fingers touch—and place yourself into another world, the world of faith. In that world you must accept the Word of God, or you won't make it there. You must know that God is truth; He is not a liar. If God says it, it is just that way.

Moses walked in that realm of faith where God's Word takes precedence over what the eyes see. The waves of the Red Sea splashed horizontally against the land at his feet. It took a strength and a force for him to say, "Waves, stop going east and west! Go vertically right now! I'm ready!" They had to obey him.

"Oh," someone says, "I don't believe that really happened."

Anyone who doesn't believe God could and would do that is relieved from the whole subject. He won't believe God can do miracles in his business. He won't believe God can do miracles in his home.

Even religion can bind. Some religions are so full of lies people are in complete bondage. But when you come to the Word of God, it begins with freedom, it ends with freedom, and all in the middle is freedom.

> ***When you come to the Word of God, it begins with freedom, it ends with freedom, and all in the middle is freedom.***

To operate in the realm of faith, you must accept God's Word as absolute truth, even in the midst of contradictory circumstances. The three Hebrew children did in a fiery furnace. Daniel did in a den of hungry lions. In both cases faith in God changed what the natural eyes saw and the natural ears heard. They had a relationship with God that knew Him as Absolute Truth.

You can have a relationship with God so that you can speak and it will be done. You can speak for yourself a better job or a better relationship in your home, and it will have to be because you speak with a force and a power greater than the atomic bomb.

God wants us to have a reserve of strength only He can give. Man cannot give it. Almost everything in our society is against it. Our materialistic society says trust in that which is material.

God spoke the universe into being without anything material. He spoke, and planets were. He created them with the power and strength of His mouth (Genesis 1; Hebrews 11:3).

We can operate in this realm, too.

You may not realize it, but your mouth is your downgoing or your upbringing. You are what you confess. You are what you confess in secret.

> **Your mouth is your downgoing or your upbringing. You are what you confess.**

If you say in secret, "I'm nothing," the devil jumps on your shoulder and says, "Boy, is that ever the truth! You're no good. I've been telling you that all the time."

But if you accept God's Word as Absolute Truth, you know that He says, *Beloved, now are we the sons of God, and it doth not yet appear what we shall be: but we know that, when he* [Jesus] *shall appear, we shall be like him* (1 John 3:2).

That's a different world—the world of faith which can change your world.

3. Realize that faith is an act

Faith is not hope. You can *hope* to be a millionaire and die a pauper. But you cannot have *faith* to be a millionaire and die a pauper. Hope folds its hands and dreams, but faith is not the same as hope. Faith is an act. With faith there is always movement.

Faith says, "I have faith for a million dollars. I'll pick up a few here, and I'll take a few there. (Hey, it's growing!) And I'll take a few more here."

Hope sits on a stool and says, "I'll just sit here, and God will do something."

When you have faith, you have action. Faith begins an operation in God.

Faith is a force living within you. It's not really you. It's something else—something good, something precious, something wonderful, something God wants you to have.

Faith is more than an idea, more than an emotion.

I don't know that Abraham "felt" a spiritual thing between Beersheba and Mt. Moriah as he took his son to offer him up. I do know the devil tormented him every step of the way. But Abraham had a thing in him called faith, and that faith was walking. It was moving and going the right direction. Faith built the altar. It laid the wood on the altar. It placed the fire upon the altar. Faith reached for the son of promise to make him the sacrifice. Movement!

When God saw that tremendous movement, He said: "Stop! I've provided a ram in the thicket for the sacrifice. Now look around to the north country a few hundred yards. That's Golgotha. Look at those three crosses."

They weren't there yet, but that was what faith had to see because Jesus said, *Your father Abraham rejoiced to see my day: and he saw it, and was glad* (John 8:56).

Abraham saw God give His Son because Abraham acted in faith.

Faith is an inexhaustible subject. I'm trusting this book will help you know faith better than I know faith, that you will begin where I leave off and build on the structure of knowledge God has poured through my being.

2
Obtaining Faith

I sincerely believe it is possible that no human ever has delved into the depths of the potentialities of faith. That means it's an open door for you and me to reach into.

It is so natural to lean upon that which is nearest to us, our flesh. It is so natural to rely upon our minds; it's so close by, so available. But to reach into the realm of faith is to reach into that which is unknown. God did not give Abraham a road map. Every day Abraham had to say, "Which way, Lord?" Yet the faith life is the greatest life on earth.

I would not write some of the things I'm sharing in this book, except we are living in the last days. God said through the Prophet Daniel that people who know their God shall be strong and do exploits in the last days (Daniel 11:32). God also said through Joel and Peter that in the last days He would pour out of His Spirit upon *all flesh.* We are about to witness the greatest display of God's power that man has ever known. God is looking for people who believe His Word.

Teaching the faith life shakes up some people. They don't want to live there. They want to live as close to material security as they can. But what will happen if it's all washed away?

I believe I'm saying this prophetically: It is God's time for faith to work. It is God's time for His miracle power to proceed.

Here are some primary principles you need to know for faith to function properly in your life.

How to Obtain Faith

The Holy Spirit through the Apostle Paul said, *So then faith cometh by hearing, and hearing by the word of God* (Romans 10:17). So faith comes out of the Word of God.

Faith does not come from philosophy. Philosophy is related to the human, which is related to the Adamic curse and the fallen nature. Philosophy cannot bring you into unadulterated truth.

Jesus said to Simon Peter, *Flesh and blood hath not revealed it unto thee, but my Father which is in heaven* (Matthew 16:17).

Only God can give information man does not have. Jesus had just asked, *Whom do men say that I the Son of man am?* (v. 13).

Some said, "John the Baptist." That's spooky—they'd just cut off his head.

Some said, "Elijah." He'd already run his course.

God doesn't do duplicates. There was only one Moses; there never will be another. There was only one Elijah; there never will be another. There is only one Lester Sumrall. There is only one you.

God is the great individualist. Every leaf on every tree in all the world has something different from any other leaf. He's a Master. This simply means that you will be a person with unique faith. Nobody will have faith like you have faith, if you reach for it, grasp it, and walk in it in Jesus' name. Living faith is obtained individually by individuals from their living relationship with God and His Word.

> *Living faith is obtained individually by individuals from their living relationship with God and His Word.*

Testimonies related to faith inspire us. But they do not generate that force and power it takes to do the job in our own lives. That comes only out of the Word of God—by reading it, absorbing it, letting it come alive within us.

The Word of God cannot build faith within us unless we permit it to become a part of our spiritual being. It cannot be just part of our repertoire of things we've read. Some people have memorized the Bible, but they don't live good lives. Memorization of the Bible, having it in their heads, is not sufficient. The Word of God has to become a working thing—working through the born-again spirit man inside you, even out through your blood system and muscle system. When the Word of God begins to work in that way, it becomes what we call faith. It becomes part of our being. So we don't just read the Bible like we read a novel or a newspaper and expect faith to come.

Jesus said, *If ye abide in me, and my words abide in you, ye shall ask what ye will, and it shall be done unto you* (John 15:7). It's not just hearing the words of the Bible; it's having the Word abide in our inner being.

Some people just pray for faith. I did that for a long time and didn't get anything. Faith does not come by praying for it.

The obtaining of great faith is not an instantaneous thing as some would like for it to be. Faith is a way of life. People look at Smith Wigglesworth's ministry and say, "Oh, he was a man who had faith," as if the Lord had given him some almost magic power. Faith is more than a display of the power of God.

> **The obtaining of great faith is not an instantaneous thing...Faith is a way of life.**

I personally knew Smith Wigglesworth. We worked together. We prayed together. I visited him many times in his home in Bradford, England. He was a man of such deep devotion you could hardly get to him—spiritually, I mean. He was so far out in front of you. I never heard him say one little thing against another human. He disciplined himself so that if he had anything to say about a person, it had to be good. He didn't do that by making up his mind to do it; he did it because of what was in his heart.

You can try and try to make yourself live right—and it's hard. Once in a while you say, "Whew! I'd like to be a little bit mean just to feel good." That's not what we're talking about. A person living the life of faith does right because doing right is what he wants to do. It's his real personality. It's the flow of God within him.

Faith can be that way in you. Faith can become so automatic within you that fears, phobias, and misunderstandings don't work. They're not a part of the structure God wants you to have.

> **Faith can become so automatic within you that fears, phobias, and misunderstandings don't work.**

God wants each of us to obtain faith through the living Word and to do what the Word tells us to do.

How to Retain Faith

God wants us to retain the faith we get. Some people are like sieves. You can pour in blessings two or three times a week, but they're always empty. God not only wants us to *receive* faith, He wants us to *contain* faith. It's not the faith I *did* have; it's the faith I *do* have.

There is more to faith than reaching out for something. Faith must become a part of our flesh and bone, spiritually speaking. It must become so related to us until we not only *did* have it; we *do* have it. We keep our faith by walking in the ways of God every day and by dispelling fears.

There is a pattern I live by. If the devil says, "Don't go in that room, there's a boogie man in there," I don't open the door—I kick it down! I let him know immediately that he's a liar and that I'm not afraid of that door. If you allow the devil to bring fears into you, that's the absence of faith. Faith cannot dwell where there is fear. To have the perfection of God's faith, there must be no fear of the past, present, or future. All fear must be gone.

> *To have the perfection of God's faith, there must be no fear of the past, present, or future. All fear must be gone.*

You keep your faith by maintaining a relationship with God so that you look with the eye that sees the invisible. Anyone can see the visible; you have to see the invisible. Abraham looked for a city with foundations whose builder and maker was God. He saw the invisible. Nobody else could see it.

People of faith get on other people's nerves. My mother was a woman of faith. She spoke into being things that were not. It irritated some people because they couldn't see what she knew she was going to get; and because they couldn't see it, they didn't want to believe it.

The power of faith is the ability to see that which does not exist. It is the ability to see that which the natural man cannot see.

When we returned from the mission field a few years ago, we had nothing. When I say nothing, we had less than that—we were at double zero! We had given away a church in this country and a church in that country, so we were at zero.

Then one of my best friends, a minister of the gospel, walked up to me and said, "Lester, you're fifty and you're finished!"

It made me so angry I said, "You're a liar!"

Then I had to talk with Jesus about it. He said, "No, you're not finished. You haven't gotten started yet. Get busy!"

So I did!

Since then there has come into being our church and the work in South Bend, Indiana, that reaches around the world through books, CD and DVD, personal teaching and ministry, and most amazing of all perhaps, the television ministry.

God did it all. Many are being helped and blessed today, and God gets all the glory for it. But I had to see those things when they were not there. When God said to me, "You're going to win a million souls," I'd say, "Yes, God. I believe it! We are!" I couldn't shrink back and say, "I've never seen a million souls." If I had, we'd never get them.

Faith is the realistic power of God that says, "I have the eye that sees the invisible." No one ever yet has beheld the fullness of what God can bring to pass through the fulfillment of faith if we continue to see the invisible.

But I want to make something plain: if it is for selfishness, it won't work. Jesus made no bread for Himself; He made loaves for the hungry. He fed at one time five thousand men plus women and children. They gathered up twelve baskets of fragments. Yet we cannot find where He took one bite.

You cannot work in this faith realm with the supernatural by saying, "I'm going to make it for myself." You'll miss it. Oh, God will give you plenty. God is a good God. But if you go after it selfishly, you will be working in another domain—another world. God may want you to work there. God may be pleased with you there, but it is not the world we're talking about where God does things that are beyond yourself.

Retain your faith by continuing to see with the eye of faith. If you can't see it, you can't have it. You can only have it if you see it.

> *Retain your faith by continuing to see with the eye of faith. If you can't see it, you can't have it.*

Retain your faith by continuing to hear with the ear that hears the inaudible. Nobody hears it except you. To you it's like thunder. You say, "Can't you hear it?" Others say, "I don't hear a thing." Our natural ear hears our neighbors and friends, but the ear of faith hears what God says. It's listening to another world. Faith hears that which natural man cannot hear.

Faith is the power to possess things that are beyond our natural capabilities. Faith is a strength to feel that which the average person cannot feel. When we are ready to move into that kind of world, God is ready to move in there with us to let the strength, power, and force of faith come into being.

How to Release Faith

To be effectual, faith must be released.

Joshua released his faith, and the walls of Jericho fell. He and the children of Israel acted on the Word of God. At God's command they marched silently around the walls once each day for six days. On the seventh day they compassed the city seven times, then the priests blew their trumpets, and Joshua commanded the people to shout. At the sound of the trumpets and the shouts of the people, great stone walls crumbled!

They didn't even fall the right way. When a wall falls, it falls outwardly. Archaeologists have discovered that these walls fell inwardly. Some have said it looks as though a superhuman force drove them into the ground. Get the angels of God pushing things around, and they can push them down and in as well as out.

31

Hundreds of thousands visit the old walls of Jericho every year. Every time some guide gives his speech, he's really saying, "God lives! God is big! God is great! God did it! This is where the walls fell inwardly!"

Yet Joshua had to have the faith to do the marching, even to do the ridiculous. I have the saying in the front of my Bible: "If I am willing to do the ridiculous, God is ready to do the supernatural."

Most people don't want to do the ridiculous. They say, "What will my neighbors think?" When people are afraid of their neighbors, they're not in the faith picture at all.

Remember that your neighbor's head is a poor place to keep your joy. I'd rather keep my joy—put there by Jesus—in my own heart.

The greatest feats in history are the feats of faith. Take Daniel in the lions' den for instance. How would you like to have been his guest that night? I can assure you those lions never had such a sweet night. It was so peaceful. Daniel knew the powers and the forces of faith released.

Second Kings 6:1-7 relates a remarkable feat. One of the sons of the prophets was felling a beam when an axe head flew off the handle into the river and sank to the bottom. The young student cried to Elisha, *Alas, master! for it was borrowed* (v. 5). Elisha cut down a stick, cast it into the water, and the iron axe head floated to the top.

It was a power beyond nature—contrary to the laws of gravity. Until you're willing to fight against the laws of nature, you're not ready to release faith.

"Oh," people say, "that's just how it is. That's just natural."

Faith is not limited to the natural process of things. I am a supernatural light. I was raised up from tuberculosis when the doctor gave me two hours to live. That was two hundred and forty thousand hours ago! We don't have to live by things that are natural. We can live by things that are supernatural in the power of God.

> **Faith is not limited to the natural process of things.**

The outflowing of faith is based on God's Word beyond natural processes and beyond one's natural experience.

The Lord Jesus once told Peter to catch a fish and take money out of its mouth (Matthew 17:27). If He had told a farmer or a bookkeeper to do that, it would have been interesting—but to tell a fisherman!

Most would say, "I've had my fist in the mouths of a million fish, and I've never pulled out a coin yet."

That's where faith comes in! It doesn't matter what your experience is—we're talking about something beyond experience.

Some might say, "Well, that's not the way I've found it. That's contrary to the law of supply and demand. That's not how you get money."

If Peter had talked like that, he would not have had a miracle. The law of supply and demand says: "Take a hook. Catch a fish. Take it to the market. Sell the fish. Have money." Peter didn't do that. He caught a fish—the first fish, not the second or third—not to eat it or sell it, but to take a coin out of its mouth sufficient to pay two men's taxes.

I know someone there that day thought he was crazy. But he acted on the Word of Jesus contrary to the nature of things and to his own experience.

The force and power of faith does the unusual.

Another time Peter had fished all night and caught nothing (John 21:3-6). Jesus said, "Try one more time. Put your net on the right side of the boat." Natural experience would have said to Peter, "All day and all night! I'm not going to throw that net in anymore." But he didn't go by his natural experiences. He obeyed Jesus, and he caught more fish than he'd ever seen at one time.

Faith can bring to you more than you will ever be able to get any other way, no matter how clever you are. It can bring dividends you've never dreamed of. It can bring great blessing to your life. It can bring joy. It can bring peace. It can bring the supernatural. It can bring God to you.

3
What Is Faith?

Faith is a force moving deep down in your spirit.

It is possible to grasp a head knowledge of faith without faith actually being a part of your inner being. Please get that. Many have a mental concept of faith, but it hasn't been born in the inner person. Faith must be born in the spirit of man before it is effective.

Man is a three-part being—spirit, soul, and body (1 Thessalonians 5:23). The mind is a part of the soul. Man's soulish nature, his mental faculties, can give assent to a principle of truth before his spirit comes into possession of it.

Christian parents, for example, can teach a child the facts of Christianity before they are born within his heart. You ask the little fellow, "Are you a Christian?" He replies, "Yes." "How do you know you are a Christian?" "Mommy told me so." That does not make him a Christian. He is a Christian when he is born again on the inside.

A seminary professor can elaborate on a biblical truth and the science of that spiritual truth to students who receive the facts in their minds, but not in their spirits. So all they have is head knowledge of that truth.

Faith to change the world is an inner force—a power beyond ourselves; a power not just ascribed to in the outer court of our minds, but born alive in the inner court of our spirits.

God alone is the giver of such faith:

For I say, through the grace given unto me, to every man that is among you, not to think of himself more highly than he ought to think; but to think soberly, according as **God hath dealt to every man the measure of faith** (Romans 12:3).

God specifically says that to "every man that is among you" (every Christian) He has given a starting point in faith. We don't have to generate the first little bit. God gives to each of us a measure of faith with which to begin. What we do with it after that is our own prerogative. How it grows and increases has to do with the way we handle it—not with God. God gives us the starting place. It is up to you and me to pursue it and say, "This faith—I love it! I like it! I will cause it to grow!"

For by grace are ye **saved through faith**; *and that not of yourselves: it is the gift of God* (Ephesians 2:8).

We come to God through faith—through an instrument of belief, of trust, of accepting. Yet many get that far and close the door saying, "I've got it all." No. They just got in the door. The treasure is on the inside. They haven't reached the heaps, and heaps, and heaps.

Not only do we initially come to God through faith, but all other manifestations of the majesty and glory of God come the same way.

> ***Not only do we initially come to God through faith, but all other manifestations of the majesty and glory of God come the same way.***

I am crucified with Christ: nevertheless I live; yet not I, but Christ liveth in me: **and the life which I now live in the flesh I live by the faith of the Son of God,** *who loved me, and gave himself for me* (Galatians 2:20).

What a tremendous statement! He had died to everything that was Paul. He had died to earthly ambitions. He had died to the seeking of personal treasure. He said: "I am crucified. Just as Christ gave up His all on the cross, I have given everything. Nevertheless I live; yet not I, but Christ liveth in me. And the life which I now live in the flesh, I live by the faith of the Son of God." He would not have been able to say, "I am crucified with Christ," except by this strength, this power, this force, this anointing called faith. Faith was the force and power of coming into such a life. For he said, "I live it by the faith of the Son of God."

*I am come a light into the world, that **whosoever***

believeth on me should not abide in darkness (John 12:46).

Faith is a power that removes darkness. When we believe, darkness is dispelled—darkness of superstition, of misconception, of error. When we get faith in our lives, we get on the truth road. Faith brings us out of any kind of darkness into the glorious truth of God. We are the children of light. Faith is the place of light. When we move in faith, we move into light. God wants us to live in the light.

*Therefore being **justified by faith,** we have peace with God through our Lord Jesus Christ* (Romans 5:1).

We are justified by faith. Justified means "just-as-if-I'd" never sinned. We are made clean before the Lord by faith—not by crawling on our knees or doing penance. We are brought into a relationship with God by the power of faith. We are justified by belief. That makes faith such a strong thing.

*Who are **kept by the power of God through faith** unto salvation ready to be revealed in the last time* (1 Peter 1:5).

You ask, "How do I live for God?"

Our security is in faith. We are kept every day by the power of God through faith. It is our faith that retains within us the strength to say *no* to the devil and *yes* to the Lord Jesus Christ.

*And **his name through faith in his name** hath made this man strong, whom ye see and know: yea, the faith which is by him hath given him this perfect soundness in the presence of you all* (Acts 3:16).

Faith in the name of Jesus had brought about a mighty miracle. When we have faith in the name of the Lord Jesus Christ, we can expect the miracle power of God to function. Faith is a power.

> ***When we have faith in the name of the Lord Jesus Christ, we can expect the miracle power of God to function.***

No Condemnation

When you get into this message of faith, you can, if you don't watch it, bring yourself into condemnation by thinking, *I don't have the faith I ought to have.*

Faith is not a condemnation message.

Remember, faith is a growing thing (2 Thessalonians 1:3). Rather than saying you don't have enough, dig around what you have. Make it grow. Rather than saying you don't have enough, add something to the faith you have on the principles of faith you will learn in this book.

The goals of faith are challenging, but never discouraging. When people say, "I'm discouraged about faith," they're not working in faith; they're working in something else. We're not talking about something that makes you sad; we're talking about something that makes you glad!

Don't speak negatively about the amount of faith

you have. If you have any, you're blessed! So take what you've got and start using it. When you have a dollar in your pocket and you need five, you don't curse the one you have. You say, "I've got one. Thank God for that."

You do have a measure of faith. Learn how to use it progressively and productively to make it come alive and bless the world.

Faith Defined

Faith is like life and like love. Life and love are indefinable but enjoyable. You may not be able to define an egg, but you can enjoy it. You may not be able to define faith completely and absolutely, but you can certainly enjoy it. It is as enjoyable as white milk from a black cow who ate green grass. You may not be able to follow the line and interpret everything that happened, but the milk tastes good. So it is with faith. Faith is refreshing, alive, light, glorious. And we must have it.

Faith is the greatest power generated on the planet earth and is the number one source of unused energy. That to me is a terrible thing. Unused power! If just the people reading this book would wake up every day and say, "I will release my faith today. I will release my trust in God today. I will release the force Abraham and Moses had within them. I will release the thing that kept Joseph alive in prison for ten years. I will release it today," an absolutely invincible power and force would be released in the earth.

Faith is positive. Faith knows. Faith is sure. If you

don't have that aspect of it, it won't work for you. But it wants to work. It wants to work in your life and mine. Most of our troubles come because we doubt, or falter, or say maybe. When you get into that area, you are not in faith. If you are not sure that you're sure, you are not in the area of faith.

Faith flows from God. It is the divine essence. Both faith and love flow from the heart of God. If you can get hold of both of them, you will have life upon this earth without limitations.

> ***Both faith and love flow from the heart of God. If you can get hold of both of them, you will have life upon this earth without limitations.***

I told a group of Bible school students: "Doctor Oral Roberts began as a poor person. His father was a humble preacher of the gospel. Yet through a strength called faith, hundreds of millions of dollars have come through his hands. He had nothing natural to bring it about, no human relationships. It was the sheer strength of inward faith. He commanded that thing to come alive."

But don't begin on the wrong end of faith. Faith is a life.

A young pastor of a little church came to me so frustrated he didn't know what to do. He said, "I'm ashamed to see my people. Last Friday I stood and prophesied that by the next Monday I would have a house and it would be paid for. Monday came and I didn't have anything. I'm scared to go back to church."

"Sit down," I said. "Had you ever prophesied before?"

"No."

I said, "Why didn't you keep it to yourself then? Test it one time. Every car on the road was tested before it came out of the factory. You're still in the factory. Why didn't you give it one test?"

Give it a test. Before you tell the Lord you want a seven-tiered cake, get a doughnut out of Him.

> *Before you tell the Lord you want a seven-tiered cake, get a doughnut out of Him.*

The devil wants to destroy you, you see. He wants you to ask for something beyond your faith so he can stop you.

Our faith toward God must be simple. Take it layer upon layer, blessing upon blessing, anointing upon anointing. Tomorrow you believe for something you could not believe for today, and you reach out.

If I had not left my home when I was seventeen with 65 cents, I would not be able to serve God as I am today. If I had not left this country in 1934 with only $12 to go around the world and preach the gospel, I would not have a television station today. But if you had told me in those days to buy a television station, I'd have run so fast I'd have been in Africa before you caught up with me! I wasn't ready for it.

We have to get ready for things. That's what this book is all about—to teach how to be ready for what God wants to do for us.

I believe you are reading this book because you want to be ready. I believe you want faith to change the world. But you have to set your spirit to it and say, "Lord, I'm going to learn it every day. And I'm going to move with it. And when it doesn't seem to work, I'm not going to accuse God. I'm going to say, 'Devil, where are you? You're messing around here somewhere. You get out of this. I rebuke you. Go!'"

Don't blame things on God. Blame them on the one who causes them. Resist the devil; he will flee from you, and you will have victory (James 4:7).

Subtle, Simple

Faith is the most subtle power on earth because natural man cannot see it. It slips up on him. What person living in Ur of the Chaldees would have believed that by traveling up the fertile crescent to another land Abraham could become such a hero of faith that four thousand years later the whole world would be talking about him?

Faith is a tremendous force. If it were easy to handle and easy to define, many more people would have it.

Yet we say faith is simple. And it *is* simple. But it is "simple-complex." Men who work in electronics tell me electronics is simple. I appreciate what they say. But when I consider the electronics maze I think, *I'm glad somebody understands it. I don't. I'm just blessed that I can put on a microphone.* We don't want faith to be that way in your life. We want faith to be reduced to simplicity as far as we can.

If I were a person of no experience, I would have to write this book in an academic way from what others have said and done. But this is not an academic presentation. Faith functions in my life.

Wherever I go, people ask, "Will you teach me about your faith?" I am taken by surprise because I don't feel that way about myself. But whether I especially like it or not, this generation has branded me as a person of faith. If that be true, we had better study the subject together. We had better look into it and discover all the things that should be discovered and put them into action to change ourselves first, then our families, our communities, our nation, and then the world. This is God's business, heaven's business, faith's business.

4
Faith Unlimited

Faith has no limitations. **You** are the only person who can limit faith in your life.

It is the devil who wants you to say: "My wife is to blame." "My husband is to blame." "My parents are to blame." "My children are to blame."

No! **You** are to blame! You are the possessor of your own faith. You are the extender of your faith. You are the projecter of your faith.

Faith knows no limitations! It is possible that no human, including Moses and Abraham, has gone to the perimeter of the possibilities of faith in his own life. That means every human who ever lived could have gone further had he wanted to, had he given himself to it, had he permitted his insides to reach out again and again, saying, "I'm reaching for something."

You usually get what you reach for. Check and see what you have, because that's what you've reached for up to this moment. But from this moment you can reach for something huge. Faith knows no limitations! You are not limited as to what you can receive through the power and force of faith! God has placed no limitations to confine you in any area.

> **Faith knows no limitations! You are not limited as to what you can receive through the power and force of faith!**

All you can believe for, you can obtain. You can get it if you will say, "Lord, I will not be limited. I will not be limited by my own thinking. I will not be limited by my own feelings. I will release myself under the structure of faith. And I will have it." Then you will get it.

No Boundaries

Faith knows no boundaries. We often think faith has walls. It does not. The power and blessings of God refuse to be circumvented, held down, or held back by boundaries.

Faith knows no racial boundaries. Chinese, African, European—God loves everyone equally. The Bible was written through people we call Asians, not by north Europeans. So the Bible is not a European book. Neither is it an Asian book. It is a God book!

Faith knows no economic boundaries. It is just as wonderful for a child to ask God for a dollar and get it as it is for a father to ask God for fifty and get it. Both are an answer and a movement of divine faith.

The poorest can have faith. People often think, *Because I am poor, I can't do this or that.* That's a lie! Some of those who have accomplished the greatest economic feats began with no securities of any kind.

They created something as they moved through the principles of faith. Nothing could hold them back.

The wealthiest can have faith. A man with fifty million dollars can put faith to work just as easily as someone can with two dollars. It makes no difference with God.

Wherever you are on the economic ladder, don't compare yourself with others saying, "I'm going to get as much as he has." That's not the system. It is your believing God for what you need in that specific moment. If you compare yourself with others and say, "I'm going to get what he's got," then God may say, "But that's not good for you. That won't bless you. Let Me bless you with what you need." Turn your faith loose in your own life. Then faith works.

Faith knows no social limitations. God can bless socialites and cause them to meet and influence people. God can bless convicts and make them a blessing in jail. It does not matter where you are socially. In your home faith can work. On your job faith can work. In the hospital faith can move. In the prison house faith can move. Faith invades and pervades all societies. Faith is not limited to anyone, anywhere. You can take it wherever you go.

No religion can make a boundary for your faith. Faith jumps religious fences. Some think that unless you belong to a certain group you cannot move in faith. That is not true. A Catholic can have faith. A Presbyterian can have faith. A Pentecostal can have faith. You can belong to any group and have faith. Or, you can belong to those same groups and have nothing. The source of life and faith is not any group; it is God. God recognizes no denominations. God reacts to people. Jesus loves people. He wants to bless people. And He wants to increase your faith.

> ### The source of life and faith is not any group; it is God.

The powers of faith will never be circumscribed by anything human, anything natural, anything economic, anything sociological, anything religious, anything denominational. Faith knows no boundaries! Now if you won't get that, you won't get faith. If you don't believe that, you won't ever have faith.

Faith refuses to sit underneath while someone sits on top of it. Faith is a runner. It's a leader, always in front. To stay up with it, you have to move with all of your might.

Faith refuses to recognize boundaries. So in faith you love everybody. You accept the power of God wherever it is.

Some say, "Oh, that's not the power of God. It didn't happen in my church." What does someone's church have to do with it? Nothing. Absolutely nothing.

The power of God is God's love, and God's love is everywhere. Open your spiritual being and say, "Lord, I'm going to trust. I'm going to have the right attitude. I'm going to learn."

Remember, faith has no limitations. (That's big!) You set all the boundaries your faith has. Cut them loose! Break them down! Burn them up! Then faith can move in areas you never before realized.

No Compromise

Faith accepts no compromise.

Politics compromise. Many religions compromise. Tens of thousands of pastors preach what they know people like. But faith knows no compromise.

When you get into a feeling of compromise, you are not in faith. You're in doubt and in fear. Faith knows no fear.

Let the waves roar! Christ says, "Peace. Be still."

Let the demoniacs scream! Christ says, "Sit down. Give him a coat. He's naked. It's all taken care of."

Faith refuses to say, "I'll do this if you'll do that." Faith moves without compromise. It knows the truth. It lives in truth. It projects truth.

> *Faith moves without compromise. It knows the truth. It lives in truth. It projects truth.*

Faith is right in the middle of the Word of God! Faith knows no arbitration.

Faith doesn't "deal." You don't say, "Listen, I'll have a little faith if you'll have a little doubt mixed in." God says, "No. Nothing doing. Faith is pure."

Some denominations compromise to fit the times

in which they live. Faith is the same today as it was in Abraham's day.

In all the operations of faith recorded in the Bible, there are no failures. The three Hebrew children didn't come out of the fiery furnace scorched. Faith works. Faith succeeds. The Bible records no defeats related to faith.

There is no cowardice related to pure faith. The history of the martyrs shows that faith dies joyfully. Faith sings on its way to the burning flames of persecution.

John Bunyon was imprisoned twelve years for preaching on a street corner. Out of his dungeon prison came what may be the most powerful book ever written, except the Bible, *The Pilgrim's Progress to Heaven.*

Faith knows only superb fulfillment.

Faith lives in joy. If you're not happy, you may not be in faith at all. It may be doubt. It may be fear. Faith lives in total joy. Faith sings in your heart, no matter what assaults your soul.

You may say, "My, what a lot of words about faith."

I say, "No tongue has ever been able to give the full and complete definition of faith."

5
Faith Measured

There are degrees of faith. There are measurements of faith.

The Word of God teaches that every man is given "the measure of faith" when he is born again (Romans 12:3). After that his "measure of faith" is his to do with as he wills. Some people, ten years later, still have the same amount, or less. They have done nothing with it. Though this is often the case, it is subnormal behavior according to God's will for the Christian. His plan for our spiritual lives calls for development and growth of the measure of faith.

Faith grows and develops in the same ways our physical bodies grow and develop—by eating good food and exercising properly. The food that faith thrives on is the Word of God (1 Peter 2:2; Romans 10:17), and the faith in our hearts is to be exercised through regular use.

> *The food that faith thrives on is the Word of God, and the faith in our hearts is to be exercised through regular use.*

Every day that you don't use faith, it shrinks. If

you were to leave your legs unused, they would weaken and diminish in size. So it is with faith. Faith is a commodity for use. It is not something to be put into a little golden box with the lid snapped shut while its owner announces, "I've got faith!" Faith is of no value to us unless it is used.

The Bible gives several measurements of faith. Here are some of them:

Weak Faith

And being not weak in faith. . . (Romans 4:19).

Sometimes we discriminate because a person doesn't have a lot of faith. We push him down. If he's got any faith at all, thank God for it!

Yet I am sure there are times when God wants to do something of a tremendous nature through men who are not able to do it because of the weakness of their faith.

Don't let your faith be weak. Let your faith do something that will make it strong.

Little Faith

And when he was entered into a ship, his disciples followed him.

And, behold, there arose a great tempest in the sea, insomuch that the ship was covered with the waves: but he was asleep.

And his disciples came to him, and awoke him, saying, Lord, save us: we perish.

And he saith unto them, Why are ye fearful, O ye of little faith? Then he arose, and rebuked the winds and the sea; and there was a great calm (Matthew 8:23-26).

They had faith; they were out there! Most of the folks weren't even there. We laugh at them and say, "Oh, they didn't have much faith," when we weren't there.

Sometimes we ridicule a man because he doesn't exercise faith; but if we were in his boots, we might be in the same mess! He may be going through something harder than we've been into yet. Don't hasten to down him. If he's got a little faith, say, "Lord, help him to add some more to the faith he has. Help him to do something with it."

Thank God for the "little faith." But don't stay that way. Let your faith grow.

Growing Faith

We are bound to thank God always for you, brethren, as it is meet, because that your faith groweth exceedingly. . . (2 Thessalonians 1:3).

Here we find a growing faith. Your faith can increase until the time you go home to be with God. Every day of your life talk to yourself and ask, "Am I growing in faith? Is my faith growing?" If it isn't, work on it.

Faith grows with proper food and exercise.

Strong Faith

He [Abraham] *staggered not at the promise of God through unbelief; but was strong in faith, giving glory to God;*

And being fully persuaded that, what he had promised, he was able also to perform (Romans 4:20, 21).

Thank God for strong faith! It just stands like a mountain. It stands, and stands, and stands!

> ***Thank God for strong faith! It just stands like a mountain.***

Great Faith

The Lord Jesus said that a certain person had great faith. That's certainly better than weak faith or little faith.

And when Jesus was entered into Capernaum, there came unto him a centurion, beseeching him,

And saying, Lord, my servant lieth at home sick of the palsy, grievously tormented.

And Jesus saith unto him, I will come and heal him.

The centurion answered and said, Lord, I am not worthy that thou shouldest come under my roof but speak the word only, and my servant shall be healed.

For I am a man under authority, having soldiers under me: and I say to this man, Go, and he goeth; and to another, Come, and he cometh; and to my servant, Do this, and he doeth it.

When Jesus heard it, he marvelled, and said to them that followed, Verily I say unto you, I have not found so great faith, no, not in Israel (Matthew 8:5-10).

He could have said it this way, "I have not found such big faith in church. I had to go out to the pagans to find it." This man was a Roman, an officer in the Roman army.

Sometimes you find real raw faith in a place you weren't expecting to find it, in a person you didn't expect to have it. You say, "How did faith get here?" Well, faith cannot be circumscribed or circumvented. God puts faith in any heart that's open to it.

The Lord Jesus Himself marveled at this man's great faith. You say, "What was so great about it?" It was great because it believed in a word. The Jews believed in rubbing. They would douse people with oil, give them a good rub, and say, "God help you and bless you." But here was a man who believed that fifteen or twenty miles away Jesus could say, "Be healed," and his servant would be healed that moment by a word.

This great faith had to do with the electronic age we live in today, the telecommunication age, the satellite age. Just speak it and it will be performed. Jesus called that great faith—unlimited faith, faith that is not circumvented by circumstances. It's released and it's gone.

Great faith can change the world—the whole wide world!

Part II

The Continual Pursuit
of Faith

6
Faith: An Eternal Quest

Faith is a quest—a seeking you never quit. I am sure that Paul on the last day of his life was in a quest for faith. Every Christian's heart desires to possess this tremendous asset to spiritual victory. If he yields to his inner desire, it becomes an eternal quest.

I have sought faith for fifty years. I may be further along with it than I sometimes think I am, and I may not be quite as far along as I sometimes think I am. But I am giving you in a few pages what I have spent thousands of hours learning.

First, you must learn the secret of the stockpile— the place to go and get the rudiments and elements of which faith consists. It is the Word of God. *So then faith cometh by hearing, and hearing by the word of God* (Romans 10:17). If you seek faith in any other place, it will not come as pure, undefiled faith.

The Word of God declares, *Now faith is . . .* (Hebrews 11:1). Those three words stop you right there. Faith is. It is a reality, a truth, a power. Faith is. It is a reality you can get hold of.

Early in a quest for faith one discovers that above all else we must have faith in order to please God. *But without faith it is impossible to please him: for he that cometh to God must believe that he is, and that he is a rewarder of them that diligently seek him* (Hebrews 11:6). God cannot be pleased without this element of trust we call faith. Therefore we must move into it saying, "God, I am going to please You. I am going to please You by believing and trusting like those great patriots of old."

> ### God cannot be pleased without this element of trust we call faith.

To make contact with God, you need faith. If you don't believe God exists, you cannot find Him. So faith is contacting God.

In contacting God you begin to know God. Faith is also knowing God. We know God through personal experiences, every day, in line with His written Word.

I come to know God by what happens to me. If I were sick all the time, I'd wonder if He were sick. But I'm not sick all the time. I've been well fifty years. I've enjoyed marvelous health in a hundred nations of the world in all kinds of conditions.

Some who have been living this faith life a long time have experience with God that newcomers don't have yet. Sometimes a newcomer grasps for something big and claims it. When he doesn't get it, he has a shocking disappointment. But it doesn't manifest because he hasn't made these first steps of contacting God, of knowing God through experiences, and of coming into the place of spiritual maturity.

Any politician in Washington could have read the Gettysburg Address, but it wouldn't have meant much. It took Abraham Lincoln to do it. Why? Because it was Lincoln. It became immortal because of what was inside him, not because of what he said. Those words were so simple. When I read them once, I said, "Where's the greatness?" God answered me, "The greatness is not in words. The greatness is in the person who said them."

When you go out to do wonders for God, the greatness is not in what you say, but in who is saying it. When you read from the Word of God, the words may be very simple. They may be words you see in your daily newspaper. But they're not the same because of Who said them. When God says them, it makes a difference.

When a mature person who has delved into the awesomeness of faith lives and speaks in line with the Word of God, he walks roads never before trodden by men. He takes paths yet unborn. He feels what others do not understand.

To many, the paths remain untrodden. But we who are in this eternal quest for faith walk them all the time. And we enjoy them! Oh, the air of that world— so fresh! Oh, the flowers which bloom in that world— so fragrant! Oh, the fruit served in that world—so refreshing! Learn to walk in that world of spiritual maturity in God.

Faith is of the spirit of man. Life within the believer's spirit gives birth to faith. The spiritual life within begins when we first contact God. Then we know God through contacts. We make contact after contact with God. We call those contacts "experiences in God." All the while the commodity called faith grows within us to a place of spiritual maturity until we come to know more about faith than others know. We can make decisions others don't make. Others say, "Can you imagine a person taking such a chance?" We're not taking a chance. We know Him. They're taking a chance because they don't know Him. When that spiritual maturity within begins to blossom and bear fruit, one of those fruit is faith.

> *When that spiritual maturity within begins to blossom and bear fruit, one of those fruit is faith.*

So faith can mature in our spirits naturally, you might say, as a fruit. But there is a faith that is supernaturally put down inside us as a gift. The Bible calls this "the gift of faith" (1 Corinthians 12). When this happens, we move from the natural to the supernatural—a higher elevation of faith. One Christian has faith that moves in a natural way, while another's faith moves so far above that until it is obvious there is a gift of God moving in him.

Living by Faith

The Bible teaches that the just shall *live* by faith. (Habakkuk 2:4; Romans 1:17; Galatians 3:11; Hebrews

10:38). That means every day we should live by faith. Faith has to do with all the vital issues of the Christian experience. If something is an issue in your life, your home, or your work, faith has to do with it.

Some would have houses or jobs or businesses they've never had, but they didn't have enough faith to grab them. Some would have known triumphs they've never known, but they panicked. Fear struck and paralyzed them. Doubt hit. *Kerplunk!* Down they went.

Faith is to be a constant dominating experience in your life—not something that comes once in a while. Yet it is possible to have faith one day and not use it the next. In every aspect of life, faith is an element. If you overrule the element of faith in one area, then try to use it somewhere else, you won't have the measure that's necessary. If you don't let faith move in your home, it won't move in church. Faith is a strength abiding within us at all times. We must hold it fast.

> ***Faith is to be a constant dominating experience in your life.***

Continually test yourself.

If you have a quarrel with your wife or husband, ask yourself, "What would faith do about this?" Inside you, faith will say, "Ask forgiveness."

When you start to make a decision or do something, ask, "Is this faith's road I'm walking?"

"Oh, no," you might say. "This is the road of un-belief. I'm getting off this road. I don't belong here."

When you ask, "Is this faith's choice?" you'll sometimes say, "Oh, no. That's a fearful choice. I'm not making that choice. I don't want fear dominating my life."

That's living by faith. That's the eternal quest for faith. You must do it all the time. Don't quit. Just pursue it.

God's Word declares, *If ye will not believe, surely ye shall not be established* (Isaiah 7:9). In your business, your home life, all the natural and spiritual decisions you make, if you don't believe, you cannot be established. The strength of establishment, the strength of your footings and foundations, is related to faith.

The establishment of our Christian faith, our Christian security, and our Christian life is based on this element of living faith. Therefore it is imperative to first *comprehend* faith—and then to *apprehend* faith. Understand it, then get it.

> *The establishment of our Christian faith, our Christian security, and our Christian life is based on this element of living faith.*

If you seek to do this, you will not come away disappointed. No one who ever sought real faith has. Those who seek God, find God.

The World of the Sixth Sense

Faith can become to you a kind of sixth sense. As humans we contact the physical world around us through five physical senses. But the sixth sense—if faith can be called that—is beyond those five senses. It has nothing to do with physically hearing, seeing, touching, tasting, or smelling. Those physical senses make us aware of the material things around us. Faith makes us aware of God. With the sixth sense we have an awareness of Jehovah, the Most High.

Christians therefore have a sense unconverted people do not have. They have five senses that make them aware of the material world. But we have a sixth sense that makes us aware of the spiritual world—a world the natural eye cannot see and the natural hand cannot feel. That bothers some people. They don't want anything they can't see and feel. But we know that such a world—the world of the sixth sense—does exist because we can be in constant contact with that world.

Anyone who desires can contact God and have relationship with Him and recourse to the resources of that world through the sixth sense. It is available to all who will seek the Lord according to His Word.

Faith Maintenance

It is one thing to obtain faith, another to maintain it. I have witnessed people who had an unusual act of faith take place. But after that they seemed to live very natural lives. They never rose any higher in faith.

Don't have a mountaintop experience. Have a plateau life. Get up there and live. Don't get back down at all. In this book I'm not talking about faith as a peak, but as a rule of life—faith that's going to bless you every day, morning and night; faith to live with, to be refreshed in, to walk in. You won't be disappointed in this kind of faith.

To maintain faith do what the Apostle Peter wrote, *Add to your faith virtue* (2 Peter 1:5).

People don't usually relate faith to virtue. They usually relate faith to magic. But God relates faith and virtue. This is because God is a moral God. He is the Moral Majority.

There are men who think it is clever to speak against morality and to make fun of people who want to live right. Such a man is in trouble, and he'll know it soon enough. Morality is not something to smirk at. Morality is what strong nations are built with. Downgrade morality and you're on your way to hell in this world and the next one, too.

God help us to know that morality is sweet, lovely, gracious, wholesome, happiness. I'm glad I've got a share in it. How about you?

Faith adds virtue. When you've got faith, you immediately move into a virtuous situation, a clean and honest situation (Faith is never dishonest. Dishonesty belongs to the devil). You become Godlike.

You cannot have this tremendous faith living like the devil—living in fear, in hatred, in backbiting. You can't say something nasty about me, then pray for the sick in the next two minutes and get anybody healed.

> **You cannot have this tremendous faith living like the devil—living in fear, in hatred, in backbiting.**

Manifold things can be added to our spiritual being through faith. Faith is an additive. It keeps adding things to you: good things, precious things, wonderful things, Godlike and Christlike things.

New Person Faith

Faith is not a sword just to grab and cut someone with. Faith is a life. Faith goes from your hair to your toenails. It is a propelling force that moves you through this life to great victories. With faith in your heart you won't wake up in the morning discouraged. You won't wake up angry at half the world. That's not possible. Faith is a propellant. It's a motivator, a mover.

> **Faith is a propelling force that moves you through this life to great victories.**

I can't get away from that man of faith, Smith Wigglesworth. I'd heard exciting stories about him all my natural life. Then I met him in Wales in 1936. He addressed a national conference in the afternoon and I preached in the evening. When I had finished, he didn't say, "You gave a good talk." He laid his hand on my shoulder and said, "You need to come and see me." I'd been in the principal's office before, and I thought I could stand it again, so I said, "Yes, sir. I'll be there."

I not only went once, I went dozens of times. But what amazed me was that after two years of going to see him in rain, in sunshine, and in all kinds of situations, he was always the same. When you saw him once, you'd seen him. Period.

I asked him once, "How can you be like you are all the time?"

He said, "I never ask Smith Wigglesworth how he feels."

That was Smith Wigglesworth talking to Smith Wigglesworth. He was a man of faith. He got up with it in the mornings. He went to bed with it in the evenings. He used it all through the day.

In a sincere quest for faith there is a deliberate action in seeking to understand not only what faith is, but how it motivates our lives to make us a new person in Christ Jesus.

7

In Pursuit of Faith

So then faith cometh by hearing, and hearing by the word of God (Romans 10:17).

My son, attend to my words; incline thine ear unto my sayings.
Let them not depart from thine eyes; keep them in the midst of thine heart.
For they are life unto those that find them, and health to all their flesh (Proverbs 4:20-22).

The Word of God, the Bible, is the sole source of faith. Books and testimonies about faith inspire us, but they cannot bring this divine thing called faith to our hearts. It comes into our spiritual being from the Word of God.

But even the Word of God does not build faith within us unless it becomes part of our spiritual person. There have been men who quoted the Bible and lived like the devil. It's not how much you know about the Bible, but how much of God's Word becomes a part of you that will make a difference in your life.

> *It's not how much you know about the Bible, but how much of God's Word becomes a part of you that will make a difference in your life.*

You cannot just read the Bible like a novel or a newspaper and expect faith to come. Faith comes by continually putting God's Word inside you until it becomes a part of your inner man. The Word of God inside you causes faith to grow like a goodly seed. The movements of growing faith are positively motivated by reading, receiving, and understanding the Word of God. You read, you receive, you understand; and faith as a divine impulse rises stronger and stronger in your life.

Divine faith is the Word of God abiding in you. John 15:7 says, *If ye abide in me, and my words abide in you. . . .* It's not just reading a book about faith; it's the Word of God abiding in you that makes faith.

When God's Word abides in you, then. . . *ye shall ask what ye will, and it shall be done unto you* (John 15:7). Some miss this truth. They think that because they read the Word, they can get whatever they ask for. But it is the abiding Word within that causes faith to bear fruit.

Faith: Eyes and Ears of the New Man

Faith is an eye that can see the invisible. Your natural eye can only see what is visible. Faith is the eye of the spirit man that sees what is not visible to your natural person.

For example, before we owned a television station, my spiritual eye saw that we would have it and that a television ministry would grow from it. I knew it would reach the whole world. God said it would. So my spiritual eye saw it. Today what my spiritual eye saw is manifested to the natural eye.

My spiritual eye within me has seen ten thousand people delivered from Satan's power with one half-minute prayer on television. I have not witnessed that yet, but I know it is coming. I am waiting for that dramatic moment when somewhere—on my program or someone else's—ten thousand people are set free by one single prayer saying, "Be free from the power of the devil!"

Faith is an ear that hears the inaudible. Your natural ear hears what people say to you. Faith is the ear of the spirit that hears what God says.

> **Faith is the ear of the spirit that hears what God says.**

Saul of Tarsus found the Lord Jesus Christ just outside the city of Damascus when he was startled by a light brighter than the noonday sun. Three Scripture passages give the account. In one it seems as though the people accompanying Paul heard the sound of a voice. *And the men which journeyed with him stood speechless, hearing a voice, but seeing no man* (Acts 9:7). In another we see they did not understand what was spoken. *And they that were with me saw indeed the light, and were afraid; but they heard not the voice of him that spake to me* (Acts 22:9). They heard the voice, but they didn't pick up the words. It wasn't for them. They didn't have the inner working of God. Paul did.

Faith is an ear that hears what others do not hear. Sometimes when God is speaking to a man by faith, others are present, but they do not hear what God is saying to that specific person.

Faith hears and conceives what the natural man cannot conceive. Then faith bears that which was conceived and brings it to pass.

Faith brings you to a place where your eyes see the invisible, your ears hear the inaudible, and the work of God is born in the earth. Really it is the new man on the inside who sees, hears, and accomplishes the realities of the power of God.

> *Faith brings you to a place where your eyes see the invisible, your ears hear the inaudible, and the work of God is born in the earth.*

Faith is a hand that can touch the intangible. Faith possesses that which you do not possess.

The natural man doesn't understand that. But had

he been in my office when I signed my name to a piece of paper for one million dollars for WHMB in Indianapolis when I didn't have a hundred dollars in the world, he would have a better idea of what I'm talking about. My natural hand was touching a piece of paper. My spiritual hand was touching a television station.

Between the two was a million dollars I didn't have. But I knew as surely as I knew my name that I would have it, that I would have it at the proper time, that I would not be embarrassed, that I would not have to tell the banks, "I'm sorry. I don't have it."

You say, "What if I did it and it didn't work?"

You have to start at the ground. You can't start at the top. I left home as a teenager to be a preacher with only 65 cents in my pocket. You can start there if you like.

If you start at the right place, it does work. It has to work. You can tell it to work. You're the boss of it. You're the creator of it. You're so sure of it until it has to work. If you got up one morning and it wasn't working, you would rebuke it. You would say to it, "You work."

If you don't have faith, you'll say, "Just as I expected. It's not there."

If you do have faith, you'll say, "Get in here in a hurry. You've got five minutes to get in here. And I don't mean maybe!" You talk like this because you have come to a place of authority in the matter. You know that you know. You're sure that you're sure. Then it works.

Some say, "Brother Sumrall, that's unreasonable."

Certainly. That's what I'm talking about—that which is not reasonable. The natural man can reason, but he cannot know how this works.

It wasn't reasonable three thousand years ago that God spoke to one little man named Abraham and said, "Through you all nations of the earth will be blessed." In the natural he had two sons. One of them is the Arab people; the other is the Jewish people. One has the oil; the other has the gold. God's blessings are tremendous.

If God speaks something good toward you, say it every hour. I'm sure Abraham did. And his natural off-spring know until this moment they are selected by some Power outside themselves to receive heaven's blessings because one man knew God (He didn't go around worshiping sticks, stones, and pieces of mud. He worshiped the One Who made the universe. That makes the difference).

In this book I'm trying to get you—Abraham's spiritual seed—to believe God has selected you for heaven's blessings, too, and that faith is the eye that sees it, the ear that hears it, and the hand that receives it from the giving hand of God.

8
Eternal Conquest

Possibly no other message in the Bible is more exciting than that of faith because faith brings into being things that could never be brought into being any other way. Yet faith may be one of the most misunderstood Bible subjects.

For example, you could say the same words someone else said, but it wouldn't have the same meaning. As I often say, you can recite the Gettysburg Address, but that doesn't give you the power, strength, or courage of Abraham Lincoln.

Faith is not words. Words happen to be the vehicle. But faith is a living power, force, energy, and life within you that flows out spontaneously.

You don't get nervous with faith. You don't start saying, "Is it going to work?" If that's the case, you don't have faith. You have it when it flows naturally from your inner being. You know that you're sure, and it flows from you spontaneously.

Faith flows through your eyes. You have the look of faith. Depression and doubt also come out through the eyes. Your eyes can be either negative or positive. Make them positive.

Faith flows spontaneously from your mouth. You speak faith. Some think they can say anything they want, and it won't affect them. That is not true. What is in your heart proceeds out through your mouth. If you don't have faith—when you just think you have faith, or you speak somebody else's words of faith—then in your casual moments you will speak what is really in your heart. "Is that me?" you'll say. Yes. The real you. The absolute you. The only way to change that is through the words of God.

Through the Word of God you change what you are on the inside. The Bible will change your way of thinking and acting. No wonder faith comes by hearing, and hearing by the Word of God (Romans 10:17).

We're studying the eternal quest for faith. Here's a tip for your quest: Read God's Word out loud. Two things will be functioning for you at the same time: seeing and hearing.

I understand that Colonel Sanders of fried chicken fame was an older man before he struck it rich. Really, he didn't strike it rich. He put his faith into action and it worked. I trust many today won't be graybeards before they get faith working for them.

I forever remember something I said when I was twenty. I was starting off to go around the world with only $12 to my name. Someone said to me, "You won't ever get back. You'll die out there somewhere in a foreign country. You have no money to get back with."

I looked at him and said, "While I'm young, I've got to find out whether God is there or not. I don't want to wait till I'm old and still be searching around to see if God is real. I want to find out now. If He's not real, man, I'm going to have a time. But if He is real, I'm going to live for Him. I'm going to serve Him. I'm going to obey Him."

I soon learned in a phenomenal way that God loves, God cares, God provides, and that it is good serving the Lord. In foreign lands where I had no acquaintances God provided in supernatural ways far removed from being possible by incident or accident. Faith is not an incident or an accident. It is the living God flowing through you.

Words for Faith

The Greek word translated *faith* in the New Testament is *pistis.* It is used 248 times and is also translated *assurance, fidelity, belief.*

Dictionaries work at defining faith, but they are uncertain as to what it is. They usually say it is believing in something. And it is. We believe in God. We believe in the Word of God. Faith is *belief.*

It is also *fidelity.* We know that if we ask anything of Him according to His Word, He will give it. That's the fidelity part. We know we're not working with someone who can't be trusted. Many people can only be trusted at a big dinner. You'd better not trust them when you're meeting a tiger. You'll be on your own and they'll be gone. God won't leave you when you face a tiger. Your relatives may leave you. The businessmen you work with may leave you. But Jesus Christ will never leave you. God says in His Word, *I will never leave thee, nor forsake thee. So that we may boldly say, The Lord is my helper, and I will not fear what man shall do unto me* (Hebrews 13:5, 6). We can rely on His fidelity. Faith is the faithfulness of God.

Faith is *confidence.* When you believe in something, you have confidence in it. You have confidence in the chair you're sitting in. Because you believe it will support you, you can relax and read this book.

In Christ there is confidence. We relax in Him. We're not nervous. We're not saying, "Oh, is it going to happen?" That's not in the language. It's going to happen because it has always happened. In faith there is the element of confidence which brings relaxation in God. It's a matter of just leaning on Him.

Jesus is the Author and Finisher of our faith (Hebrews 12:2). He is the beginner and the ender, the giver and the protector of our faith. We're not the only ones interested in our faith. God is also interested in it. He is the Author of it. He is the One Who gave birth to it. The essence of it flows out of Him to us. Faith is not generated by man. Faith is not conceived by a preacher, a denomination, or a philosophy. Jesus Christ is the Author of faith. He is the beginner of it, and He is the protector of it. The devil can't steal it, and the world can't grab it. It's yours! It's yours because He is the One Who placed it in your heart.

> *Jesus Christ is the Author of faith . . . The devil can't steal it, and the world can't grab it. It's yours!*

Faith is a *praise* unto God. I am deeply impressed with the area of praise in faith.

A young man came to our church in Manila, Philippines, who had raised twelve people from the dead. "That's not many," he said. "There are people in Indonesia who have raised a hundred people from the dead."

Across the dinner table in our home I asked him, "Sir, how do you raise the dead?"

He said, "We say a very simple prayer: 'Lord, has this person lived out his days that You ordained? (Seventy at least.) Has he lived out his divine purpose?' If the Lord says, 'Yes,' we bury the body. If the Lord says, 'No,' we say, 'We'll stop that right now. Death, hear us. We speak to you in the name of the glorious Son of God Who rose from the dead. Death, you leave him now! His life returns. We believe it, in Jesus' name.'"

That's all they say. Then they hold hands, step back, and begin to sing. They sing until he gets up and joins them.

That's not nervous, is it? Some would want to massage him. Rubbing doesn't do any good. Some would want to yell in his ear, "Do you hear me?" No. He doesn't hear. He's dead.

These people speak the word of faith. Then they praise God.

Many times we pray for people to receive healing. Before you get two feet away from them, they say, "I'm not healed." And they're not. They never will be. When prayer was made, they should have started thanking God. "Oh, but how can I thank God when I've still got so-and-so?" they say. They'll always have it.

Faith is taking that which does not exist in the physical realm and claiming it, saying, "I've got it!" If you can't do that, then you don't have faith. Faith is that. Faith is possessing what you cannot touch with your hands. It is having what you cannot see with your eyes.

> ***Faith is taking that which does not exist in the physical realm and claiming it, saying, "I've got it!"***

While in Washington State I saw a tremendous deliverance of an Indian girl. She was terribly immoral, a harlot. She drifted in that night full of the devil and tried to tear up the meeting. She cursed me violently. I prayed for her one time, and God knocked her on the floor. Then I sat down on the altar and began to sing choruses, praising God and thanking Him for the victory. She lay there cursing, blaspheming, and saying, "I'm not coming out. I'm not coming out." We kept singing. In a few moments the power of God swept over her and swept that mess out of her. She became clean and pure. The next day she was in our morning service as changed as dark to day. It came about through one prayer and then the singing and praising of God.

Since faith is a praise unto God, that makes faith

lighthearted. If you are struggling with faith with a long face and a sad heart, saying, "I'm trying," that's not faith. You're trying something, but it's not faith. Faith never tries. Faith commands. Faith expects. Faith receives. And faith praises.

When Israel praised the Almighty, the walls of Jericho fell down inwardly and were gone.

Faith can put you on a road where you can get things you never before had. I know. I've been on that road since I was seventeen. God has always given me things I never had before.

Faith can cause you to do things you've never done before. Irregular things, things you never dreamed you would do, you start doing.

Faith can say things you never said before. Who would have the audacity to say some things we say? It's unreal. Faith puts words in your spirit that flow out your mouth until you say, "Is that me?" Faith is a strength and power that flows in words.

Faith can cause you to know God in a way you've never before known Him. Faith opens the door to realities in God.

Faith is an action. Faith is a work. To many this is a problem. They want God to do great miracles for them while they fold their hands and do nothing. "Do nothing" does nothing. When Jesus told Peter the tax money would be in the fish's mouth, Peter had to catch the fish.

When I want something, I start doing something for it. Then God does the rest. I don't sit with my hands folded and just say, "Oh, God, do a miracle." He won't.

God responds to action, to movement.

Even if I wanted a bigger job, I might take a lesser one in order to get in there and get what I want. God may want me to come through the lesser in order to get the better. Do the best you can, and you know God will do the best He can. God's best is more than enough!

Faith is when God and man choose to walk together in life, to think together, and I'd even say, to laugh together. For the faith life is the happiest life. Faith has no relationship with idleness. It has to do with a man who gets out there and goes for God, and God goes for him.

Part III

Now Faith Is!

9
Faith Revealed

The Lord Jesus told Peter, *Flesh and blood hath not revealed it unto thee, but my Father which is in heaven* (Matthew 16:17).

There are truths only God can make real. The truths I am giving you I did not read in a book, I did not study from a teacher; they were born within my spirit.

I grew up in a religious atmosphere. Yet during my youth I never remember anybody—minister or otherwise—telling me what faith is. When I began ministering as a young man, I listened to other preachers, but I met no one who could define faith in a simple language that I could understand and follow. They would say that faith is mysterious, that some have it and some don't, and we don't know why. I thought great faith was a rare gift from God for a select few, and I had missed the selection.

But I kept wrestling with the topic of faith. In my first years of ministry, I would preach on it. I would say, "Faith is wonderful, marvelous, glorious, stupendous." And it is. But faith is not adjectives.

I must have asked God for faith a million times, and I never did get anything. You can ask God the second million times, and you won't get anything either. That's not the way faith comes.

Then one night, years ago now, my life was changed. My wife and I were ministering in Puerto Rico. On Saturday evening I was heavily burdened, so I asked her to take the service while I stayed home to pray. She had been a missionary in Argentina for eight years before we were married, so she was glad to preach.

The home where we were staying had a flat roof and was about a half-block from the seaside. I climbed the ladder to the top of the house and looked out over the beautiful sea and lovely palm trees. Then I began to march back and forth across the top of the house like a lion in a cage praying my favorite prayer: "Lord, give me faith." But this time, my prayer and my life were about to change. God suddenly spoke.

"I wish you would shut up," He said.

Stunned, I stopped still to listen.

"Just go down inside the house and read your Bible. I've put it all in there. Read Hebrews, chapter 11, and you will understand what faith is."

"Do you mean it's that simple?" I said. You see, I was expecting God to knock me down with something.

I rushed downstairs and began to read the eleventh chapter of Hebrews. I read it over and over again.

The next two hours were two of the greatest of my life. As I read, illumination burst inside me like fireworks in the sky. I began to see things I'd never seen. I cried. I laughed. I got revelation. I came to know faith from God from His Word, for that's how faith comes (Romans 10:17).

> **I came to know faith from God from His Word, for that's how faith comes.**

Something came that I had never dreamed was true—but it is. I will share that with you in these next several chapters.

10
Faith's Foundations

Now faith is the substance of things hoped for, the evidence of things not seen (Hebrews 11:1).

Now faith is! It is. It's right now!

For many years in my life, faith was. It was what Moses had, what Abraham had, and what I didn't have.

But faith is not historical. Faith is now! Faith functions. Faith moves mountains now.

Two Qualities of Faith

The qualities of faith are two: substance and evidence. That's exactly what nobody thought faith to be. We thought faith was ethereal and magical—that it had to do with the air and reaching for it. God says it is just the opposite. Faith is solid. It is substance. It is evidence.

Substance can be measured and analyzed. This puts faith into an area of knowledge where we can absolutely know what faith is.

Faith is the evidence of things not seen. Faith has its evidences. It produces. Abraham believed God for a son, and he produced Isaac.

Two Basic Elements of Faith

But without faith it is impossible to please him; for he that cometh to God must believe that he is, and that he is a rewarder of them that diligently seek him (Hebrews 11:6).

A strong faith structure begins with a firm foundation. To build an Empire State Building faith, you must put your footings deep. The devil will knock you off your faith if you have little sand footings. The two colossal footings which cannot be moved by earthquakes, the devil, or anything of man are these:

1. Know there is a God.

2. Know He is a rewarder of those who diligently seek Him.

Unless you know God exists, you have no basis for faith. An infidel can't have faith. A true Marxist communist can't have faith. An agnostic can't have faith. The very basis of faith is a knowledge of God's existence.

You say, "How can I increase my faith?"

Know more about God. The secret of having more faith is to know more about God. Faith has a direct relationship with our knowledge of God.

> *The secret of having more faith is to know more about God.*

Some people in high churches know very little about God. How can they have great faith?

Who has great faith? People who have great knowledge of God.

In certain areas of Indonesia they had a phenomenal revival. I talked with Mel Tari once when he was back in the United States and asked him if the revival was still going. He said it was going strong in primitive areas.

When people with a lot of feeders in their society—radio, television, and newspapers—give all their time to these modern communications, they don't have time to commune with God.

In those primitive areas, the people just sat and read the Bible. Then when they didn't have wine for communion, they prayed over the water and God turned it to wine. They raised the dead. A group of them came to a river and said, "Lord, we have no other way to get across. Here we go." And they walked across the river.

You say, "Well, Brother Sumrall, I have never seen that."

No, but you've seen a lot of television! Those people did nothing but worship God.

You say, "Well, I'd get tired of that."

Then you don't get it. Faith is commensurate to knowledge of God.

People eulogize Smith Wigglesworth. They call him a prophet of faith. But what they don't know is he sat almost all day, every day, reading the Bible, praying, and ministering to people. If you had asked him to do something else, he would have thought you were crazy. His knowledge of God was tremendous.

When I'd visit him, he'd almost wear me out. I'd walk in his house about ten o'clock in the morning. He'd meet me at the front door. He'd grab me around both of my arms and jump up and down, shouting and praising God, with me on the inside of his arms. I was twenty-four or twenty-five; he was just over eighty. An eighty-year-old man was jumping up and down with a twenty-five-year-old man in his arms!

When he got through, he'd set me down and say, "Listen to this." Then he'd read a whole chapter from the Bible. I hadn't yet said, "Good morning." I didn't have time. He was doing all the talking. As soon as he finished reading, he'd kneel down and say, "You need a blessing." He'd lay hands on me and pray for me about thirty minutes. As soon as he got through, he'd say, "Oh, yes. Here's another scripture you need." And he'd read me another chapter. Then he'd say, "Do you have all the gifts of the Spirit? No, you don't. I'll lay hands on you again."

When his daughter called for lunch, I was so dizzy I had to be led to the table.

No wonder things happened in his ministry. He knew God exists. And he knew God would respond to his prayers.

All Christians know that God exists. Yet many don't know Him as a rewarder of those who seek Him. They know God is God, that He's the Creator of the whole world. They know that upon a throne somewhere there is a mighty God, and they think, *Oh, I wonder if He likes me? If I ask Him for something, I wonder if He would give it?*

> ***All Christians know that God exists. Yet many don't know Him as a rewarder of those who seek Him.***

A leper once came to Jesus and said, *Lord, if thou wilt, thou canst make me clean* (Matthew 8:2).

The Lord turned it around and said, *I will; be thou clean* (v. 3).

The man had it backwards. He knew Jesus had the power to heal, but he didn't know Jesus had a desire to heal.

Millions of people—religious people—live that way today. They'll say, "Yes, God is Almighty. Will He heal me? I'm not sure."

I would rather say, "Lord, I know You love me. I know You would heal me if You could."

But they don't. They say, "Oh, Lord, we know You have all power. But we don't know that You have all love."

I believe in His love more than I do His power. That's the way to believe in Him. The fact is: God *is* Love and He *has* power. It is not: God is power and He has love.

You cannot get things from God until you know God will give them to you. You cannot just say, "Thy will be done." That's not faith.

Because we know that He is a rewarder of those who diligently seek Him, we ask and receive.

We lift up our hand, and He puts down His hand.

We lift up our voice, and we hear His voice coming down.

We reach toward Him, and He reaches toward us.

This makes us people of faith!

Part IV

Faith Is . . .

11
Faith Is a More Excellent Sacrifice

By faith Abel offered unto God a more excellent sacrifice than Cain, by which he obtained witness that he was righteous, God testifying of his gifts: and by it he being dead yet speaketh (Hebrews 11:4).

I'd read this verse many times before and it had not affected me at all until that night God called me off the housetop in Puerto Rico, saying, "If you want to know what faith is, go downstairs and read it in the Word of God." As I read Hebrews, chapter 11, the divine revelation of God came to me and I came to know what faith is. In verse 4, the Lord showed me that *faith is an excellent sacrifice.* I literally saw that faith is what we do with an offering plate.

I almost didn't believe it. I was shocked. I said, "Lord, that doesn't seem right to me."

The Lord spoke quickly, "You give in relationship to the amount of faith you have. If you don't have faith to give, you cannot give."

God showed me that our spiritual lives are highly related to what we give to Him. Faith and giving go together; you cannot separate them.

> **Our spiritual lives are highly related to what we give to God.**

When a person doesn't like to give, it is because he doesn't have faith. He's not to be criticized; he's in bad shape. He's barren. Living faith doesn't function in him. Things which he cannot handle will creep up in his life because the rudiments of faith are not there. He'll need healing, for instance, which he won't be able to receive.

God's Word says, *He that watereth shall be watered also himself* (Proverbs 11:25). When you give out, something comes back. But if you don't water anybody, you won't get any water.

The Bible says Abel had faith. Abel didn't say it; God said it. In most instances, greatness within a person is something he doesn't recognize himself. He thinks he's doing his own thing, normally and naturally. People say, "My, you have faith." He says, "I'm just living for Jesus."

Nobody thought the little woman in the Bible who dropped in two of the smallest coins in the kingdom had anything but poverty, but Jesus decided she had faith. He said, "She's dropped in more than all of them" (Mark 12:43). Why did Jesus speak so highly of her? Because she gave Him the total of what she had. He looked at her back pocket and said, "Honey, you don't have anything left. You've given more than all because you gave all."

When I teach a few lessons about faith like God revealed it to me, people who once said, "I want faith," then say, "I'm not so sure of that anymore. Since I came to know so much about it, maybe I don't want faith after all."

I believe that we should understand all that faith really is. Among the things to discover is that faith is an excellent sacrifice. God said it. Faith is what we do with an offering plate. One aspect of faith is that it gives.

How did Abel's faith come? First, he had to be educated to give (We still have to be educated to give). Where did he get his education? He got it from his father, Adam.

Adam gave his two sons the Word of God. He might have said something like: "Boys, when I was naked and had no clothing, God came and took a lamb. He took the skin of that lamb and put clothes on my body. My transgression caused someone to sacrifice. If someone hadn't sacrificed, I would have been naked. This was God's way of covering my sins and giving me spiritual clothing. Now you must be covered in the same way. You must take a sacrifice and offer it to God."

Each son took a different idea about what Adam said. In the six thousand years since, people haven't changed much. There are still those who think as Cain thought, *I won't do as God says. I'll do as I please with my giving to God.*

I wouldn't be a bit surprised if Abel had said, "God wants a lamb. Let me see. . . Ah! Here's a crippled one. I'll give that one to God. I wondered what I was going to do with it."

It is easy to give God what you want to get rid of anyway.

But God said, "No, Abel, that's not the one I want."

Then Abel may have said, "Here's old Spot. He's not like the rest of my sheep. He goes rambling off by himself like a goat. I'm tired of him. Lord, I'm going to give You Spot."

God said, "Sorry, I don't want Spot. Keep him yourself. Keep on disciplining him."

"Lord, what do You want?"

"You know that little lamb whose mother died— the one you brought into your tent and fed personally to keep it alive, the one that became so white and beautiful without a blemish, the one that followed you around and stayed right with you all the time. That's the one I'll take."

"Oh, no, Lord! You can't have my baby! That's the one I. . . ."

"I know, the one you love. That's the one I'm asking for."

"Well, Lord, if that's the one, You can have it."

"That's the one I want. Bring it."

So the Bible says Abel brought *an excellent sacrifice.* And God called it faith!

You've been wondering what faith is. Faith is giving to God. I didn't say it. The Church didn't say it. **God** said it.

When a resistance rises up within and says, "No! I don't want to give to God," that's the opposite of faith. The opposite of faith—doubt, fear, and unbelief—comes from the devil.

> **The opposite of faith—doubt, fear, and unbelief—comes from the devil.**

Abel offered his sacrifice and God smiled upon it. So Abel began to shout and praise the Lord around his altar. The presence of the Lord was very strong.

Across the way his brother decided to worship. He fixed an altar and put some fire on it. He said, "Lord, are You a vegetarian?"

"No."

"Well, that's what You're going to get today. I brought You some things out of my garden. Do You like onions?"

"No."

"Well, You're going to get them anyway."

Some give what they want God to have, whether or not He likes it.

"God, how about a good cabbage? This is a big one. Do You like cabbage?"

"No."

"You're going to get one today."

Cain brought what he wanted to bring and put it upon the altar. It had no blood. He looked across at his brother and said, "God, do You see my brother? He's a bloody man."

God said, "No, he is a received man. I received

him because of the blood. The life of the flesh is in the blood. He has given life to bring life. He will have spiritual life because of what he gave to Me."

Cain said, "Well, I'm not going to give it to You." So he brought the fruit of the ground and heaped it upon the altar, saying, "There You are, God."

God said, "No, I can't bless that. I don't accept it."

It is remarkable that when some people are received of the Lord, but others are not, they get upset about it.

"She's shouting too much." Why don't *you* shout? It's all right.

"I wish they'd keep quiet." *You* can be a little bit noisy if you want.

"I don't like the way they dance." *You* can have a little dance yourself.

When someone is blessed more than they are, they say, "It must not be right. I don't have it."

Cain said, "My brother's religion is bad."

God said, "No, it's good, and I have received it."

Cain got mad! Have you ever seen any mad religious people? Cain's anger grew hot. I don't know whether he intended to kill his brother. He may just have intended to knock him around a little. But he hit him too hard. He hit him a blow on the head, and his brother was dead.

That's strange religion! It's a religion that kills. There is still some of it in the world today. Religion without Jesus Christ behind it can be murder.

Behind every problem in the world today there is a spiritual factor. The problems in the Middle East are not over land. Israel's enemies have millions of miles of land they don't do anything with. Yet they want to take little Israel and push her into the sea. Israel's land has been turned into a garden. Right across her borders are millions of miles of desert. From a plane you can look down and see where the desert ends and the garden begins.

Cain killed his brother. He showed with his actions that he did not have faith. Abel's actions showed that he did. The faith was a gift to God.

God had to show me that. I'd read this passage many times and had never seen it. When God showed me, it began to sink in. Then I began to see some people right.

I remembered a little lady in South Bend, Indiana, when we were struggling to put up the tabernacle building. She worked at a laundry. One week her salary check was in the offering. When I saw it, I went to her.

I said, "Did you get your change back?"

She said, "What change?"

"Your whole check was in the offering."

"I didn't want any change back."

"Well," I said, "you've got to live."

She said, "I'll live."

Two weeks later her whole check was in there again. I got it out.

I said, "Did you get your change?"

She said, "No. What are you doing with my check?"

"I'm the pastor here. You're a widow. We don't

want widows to suffer. God only asks for 10 percent, not 100. Did you get your change?"

"I didn't want any. The Lord told me to do it. Now please stop meddling with my giving."

And I did, for two weeks. Then that thing was in there again. So I got it out.

"Did you get your change?"

"No. I don't want any change."

"You're a widow and you've got to live."

"But we've got to have a church."

"We're going to get a church. Here's your check."

"Please leave me alone," she said. "The Lord is doing something here. I have more than ever. I've paid all my bills. The Lord through other sources has supplied all my needs. And we are building a church."

Isn't it amazing how ignorant some preachers can be? I didn't know it was a spiritual thing. To me it was the money on which she lived. To her, she was worshiping. By her giving to God, God was giving to her. By giving to God, she had more than when she kept it all. I didn't catch on until God told me about it later.

He reminded me of when we were preaching in Java. One night after the service a lot of people came to the front to be saved. One by one they left until only two men knelt at the altar besides the missionary and myself. Suddenly one of them came through to something bright. His face lit up and joy came into his heart. Even though I couldn't understand the language, I could see when he received Life. The other man received nothing.

That church received offerings in a pan back by the door. I think it was a kind of conscience thing: If you had a conscience, you'd drop something in it. (They must not have had any because there wasn't much in it!)

The man who didn't get saved walked by, looked at the pan, and went out the door and down into the street. We never saw him again. I didn't think anything about it. He just didn't give like the rest of them.

But the man who got "gloriously" saved was happy and rejoicing. He jumped up, hugged the missionary, then hugged me. When he saw that pan, he grabbed his wallet out of his back pocket. Without looking to see what was in it, he opened it and emptied it all into the pan.

I saw one man pass by the offering plate like the priest and the Levite passed by the wounded man on the other side of the road (Luke 10:30-32). Then I saw another man put it *all* in! But it didn't mean anything to me—I just laughed about it—until God brought it back to me as He taught me about faith.

He said, "What it took at the altar is what it took at the offering plate. At the altar the man had no faith to believe Me, and he didn't get saved. When he got to the offering plate, he still had no faith. So he walked out with nothing. The man who got saved had faith to receive Me at the altar. So when he got to the offering plate, he demonstrated what he had at the altar. He gave evidence of it. And I took care of him later. I gave him more than he'd ever had."

Faith is an excellent sacrifice unto God.

"I've never made one," you say.

Make it unto the Lord, and He will do something for you.

I personally want to give more—not only a gift of money, but of everything! I want to give Him my experiences of the past. I want to give Him my mind, my time, anything and everything that comes my way. I want to be a giver.

Give something—music, prayer, witnessing, speaking. Whatever it is, give it wholly, completely, absolutely, and unreservedly unto the Lord.

When you do, that **is** faith! That's not talking about faith. That's not wishing you had faith. That **is** the commodity. Faith is an excellent sacrifice unto God. And if that **is** it, and you give an excellent sacrifice unto God, then you've got faith! Aren't you glad you've got some!

12
Faith Is a Walk

By faith Enoch was translated that he should not see death; and was not found, because God had translated him: for before his translation he had this testimony, that he pleased God (Hebrews 11:5).

This is one of the most unique stories of the Bible. Yet I don't wish to deal with it in its uniqueness. I wish to deal with it from the aspect of faith. God said Enoch had faith.

Enoch did not say he had faith. We're not dealing with a man's testimony of himself. God said this man had faith and that his faith caused him to have a private, personal translation—an honor in the Bible that has to do only with three men: Enoch, Elijah, and Jesus.

Enoch had faith. What if we could call him down from heaven and talk with him?

"Enoch, God says you have faith. Please tell us: What is faith and what within you caused God to say that you have faith?"

As with most great men, a definition of themselves is difficult. They only know themselves in the natural outflowing of their own personalities. Others can see a man's greatness, understand it, and write about it. But within himself, that man is only flowing naturally. Therefore it's not easy for him to tell you he's got mercy, or goodness, or faith, or love.

Enoch would say, "This is the only thing I can tell you: I had a great-great-great-great-grandfather named Adam. He was about 600 years old when I was born (Genesis 5). Since he lived to be about 930, we lived together more than 300 years. I was a favorite of his. You know how grandfathers love to tell you about yesterday. Well, my grandfather often told me about a place called Eden, a garden of God. Nothing was there but what was fruitful and beautiful and delicious.

"Into that garden, he told me, came Jehovah. He came to walk with my great-great-great-great-grandparents. They communed and had fellowship together. My grandfather would look at me and say, 'Son, how wonderful it was.'

"I would look at my grandfather and say, 'But, Grandfather, why did God stop walking with you?'

"And he would say, 'It's a sad story. We ate of the forbidden fruit, and our spirits died within us. We lost communication with God. God has never walked with me since. I've gone now these 600 years since I left the garden without God's walking with me. It's very sad to once have walked with God and now not to walk with Him.'"

I can see the boy Enoch look up into Adam's face and say, "Grandfather, I didn't sin. You sinned."

"Yes, that's true."

"Then God will walk with me."

"Oh, I'm not sure of that, Enoch. I don't think God's walked with anybody since I saw Him last."

"But I didn't sin. *You* did."

"I know that. You can ask God if He'll walk with you. I haven't seen Him anymore."

Enoch knew Adam 300 years. That's a long time to know a man. He heard the story of the Garden of Eden many times. It was the only story worth telling. He knew it frontwards and backwards.

I can see the two of them out looking over a field. The old grandfather, just a little weary, sits down on a log.

Young Enoch says, "Tell me that story again. Tell me about the angel with the sword. Tell me about God Jehovah Who doesn't walk with you anymore."

Enoch would hear the story one more time. And somewhere down inside he'd say, "I want to walk with God."

Desire rose up in his heart. You can have the unusual through deep Holy Spirit desires. It was no accident that God walked with Enoch. Desire brought it about. His desire could have been for the prettiest girl in the country. It could have been for a new house, or many other things. But the consuming desire that rose up within him was to walk with God.

Now God hadn't walked with anybody for a long time. But that didn't make any difference to Enoch. He didn't have to know what God was doing every day. He believed he could have what God wasn't doing at all. That's what faith is all about: making the impossible possible, making the improbable probable.

> *That's what faith is all about: making the impossible possible, making the improbable probable.*

So Enoch got alone and prayed, "God, walk with me as You walked with my great-great-great-great-grandfather. Walk with me, too, please. I want You to walk with me. I desire to walk with You. Please, God, walk with me."

Nobody ever sought God without being heard. Nobody ever cried out to God without God's hearing them. Nobody ever said, "God, save me," unless God saved them. God, right this moment, wants to do tremendous, amazing, and wonderful things for anyone who will just say, "Walk with me, God." God wants fellowship more than anything else.

I don't know how long Enoch prayed. I don't know how long he called out to God. I don't know how long he said, "Oh, Lord, walk with me." I only know this: The Bible says Enoch walked with God. So I know that one day as he prayed, "Lord, walk with me," he sensed a Presence.

He said, "I never felt that before. Someone is here."

The Lord said, "Yes, Enoch. It's Me. We're going to walk together."

So Enoch and the Lord walked together. When he came back, he had a story to tell that nobody would believe. He said, "Listen, you don't have to go back to the Garden of Eden. I've been walking with God **now**."

His neighbors said, "Something's wrong with you. God's not walking with anybody."

If you ever have a fine personal relationship with God, members of your own family won't understand you. Your neighbors and your friends won't understand you. You see, they're not walking with God in the same way you are. How can they understand you? They're out of step with the One you're walking with.

Most people won't understand, but the Bible calls it faith. God's Word says Enoch had faith because he walked with God.

Measuring Faith

How do you walk with God? By faith.

How much faith do you have? How close do you walk with God?

I told you we would measure your faith. We weighed it in the previous chapter. We weighed faith with how much you give to God. If you're not giving liberally, there's a lack of faith in your life. If you're not walking with God, there's a lack of faith in your heart.

I told you we would build your faith. You can do something about it. Walk closer to God. That's not asking for faith. That's not saying, "Oh, God, give me faith." That is faith. That is the outflowing of an artesian well of life that flows up out of you because you walk with God.

But it won't be there if you walk with the world, saying, "Boy, I'm going to see every new movie. I'm going to live in the best house on the street. I'm going to push everybody down and get the best job at work." You won't have time to walk with God. You'll be so selfish you'll just walk with yourself. I don't imagine your wife or husband could even stand you. The people you work with will hate you. You may attend church on Sunday morning, but you won't be walking with God. And you won't have faith. Faith is walking with God.

If you get up in the mornings angry and screaming at everybody, you are not demonstrating that you have a bad temper so much as you are demonstrating that you don't have faith. When you walk with God, you demonstrate His nature.

I asked Smith Wigglesworth, "Wigglesworth, I've seen you dozens of times. You always look the same. Why?"

He said, "Sumrall, I never ask Smith Wigglesworth how he feels. I tell him."

This was Smith Wigglesworth talking to Smith Wigglesworth. It was a spirit talking to a soul. His spirit within him was talking to his mind, his emotions, and his willpower—telling his mind what to think, his emotions how to feel, and his will what to decide. His spirit was the king of his life, motivated by faith, for if a man ever walked with God, Smith Wigglesworth was that man.

Though I was in his presence many times, I never heard him speak one word against a person. I never heard him say, "That fellow doesn't preach well." If you criticized another brother in his home, he would say, "Please get out of my house." He wouldn't let you stay.

You see, if you are a talebearer, you're not walking with God. To say, "Have you heard the latest on Brother so-and-so," is not faith. That will drain God's strength and power out of your being, and you'll be as empty as a gourd.

Faith is a walk with God.

There is a great evangelist in this country. If I named him, you would know him. It was my privilege to be the one who picked him up and drove him to church during a crusade.

He told me, "Now, Lester, I appreciate and love you. In the mornings we can have fellowship. We can play golf or whatever you like. But after three o'clock in the afternoon, I don't speak to another human, not even my wife, until I have finished my sermon. I close the curtain to humanity and walk with Jesus. When you pick me up and take me to the pulpit, I stand and speak as a man who just heard from God."

After they'd heard him, the people would say, "Oh, he's an orator."

No! He's a man who walks with God. He prays and things happen.

People said, "Look! Look! He's a man of faith." They thought it was magical. You know, a big man saying something would happen and it happened.

It wasn't that at all. He'd just had five solitary

hours in the divine presence of Jehovah. God said that **is** faith.

I asked Smith Wigglesworth, "How do you get up in the morning?"

He said, "I put my feet on the floor, and I dance all over my room with my hands upraised."

An international evangelist. A man who ministered to tens of thousands. Wherever he went, you couldn't find an auditorium big enough for the people. The famous Smith Wigglesworth danced before the Lord for ten minutes the first thing every morning. Then he read the Word of God. Then he knelt and prayed. Then he counseled those in need and answered his mail. These were his duties every day walking with God.

The first time I went to see him, I had just gotten off the train. I was all dressed up. I had my briefcase in one hand, an umbrella over my other wrist, and the London *Daily Express* under my arm. I rang the doorbell.

Smith answered it. He looked at me and said, "What's that under your arm?"

"The newspaper."

He said, "Leave it outside."

I said, "Pardon?"

"Leave it outside. I do not permit that trash in my house. Hitler and Mussolini will soon be in hell. Why should I permit those lies in my house? Leave it outside."

So I laid my newspaper down in the bushes until

I got out of his house. I'd met a man who walked with God.

Few people have spent so much of their time talking and walking with God as this man. No wonder he was different. No wonder whole nations were shaken. They tell me in Sweden that nobody had ever shaken that nation like Wigglesworth did. They tell me in Switzerland that nobody ever had the crowds Smith Wigglesworth had. India, Africa—it was the same wherever he went.

He taught many things. One of them was that you don't have to get sick to die. And he died that way. He died in church, in a little vestry right off the pulpit. Some churches in England have the auditorium on the second floor. At age eighty-seven he had walked up the twenty or so steps to the vestry. When inside, he suddenly fell to the floor. There was no pain, no sickness, no agony. Nothing. He just slipped away to heaven. No doubt he wanted to die in the pulpit anyway, close to the thing he loved.

Men saw the fruit of his labors. But to know why they were there, one must see the sap inside the tree of life that flowed forth and produced that fruit. That is faith. It flows from a life that walks with God.

If you want living faith, then walk with God. If you are going to be worldly, you will miss it. Do what you please. I'm only telling you what living faith is. If you want faith, you can walk with God and have it. If you don't walk with God, you won't have faith.

> ## *If you want living faith, then walk with God.*

Multitudes of religious people don't walk with God. They walk with sinners. They're in love with the world, and they walk after material things. Their whole life has to do with that which is natural.

If you wish, you can isolate yourself from this world and say, "Dear old world, you've gone one way, but I'm going another." When you do, the world will call you funny names. But remember, the worst place to keep your happiness is in somebody else's head.

My happiness is not in anybody's head. What others think of me has nothing to do with my happiness. My happiness is a well of life inside that flows up out of me. When I'm with someone, I'm happy. When I'm by myself, I'm happy. My happiness has no relationship to people. My happiness has to do with God. In my communion with God I have happiness.

In any aspect of walking with the world, you cannot have God's power. You can have man's power. You can have man's pleasure. You can have all the things that belong to man. But you cannot have what is God's. Faith is God's power.

Faith is not an accident. You are not just born with it. It is a gift of God. And it comes into your life by set laws. Among these laws are: Sacrifice produces faith. Walking with God produces faith.

116

Let this become a moment of divine consecration in your life to walk with God. God calls that faith. You don't have to seek for it. You don't have to beg for it. You simply have it created within you through walking with God. What God has just rubs off on you, and you have it!

13
Faith Is a Labor

By faith Noah, being warned of God of things not seen as yet, moved with fear, prepared an ark to the saving of his house; by the which he condemned the world, and became heir of the righteousness which is by faith (Hebrews 11:7).

If we could contact Noah, we would ask him about his faith. He would say something like this: "I knew wickedness was great in the land. Sin abounded. But I kept myself pure before God. One day as I was praying, God spoke to me and said, 'Noah, I have to confide in you.'

"I said, 'Lord, what is it?'"

"He said, 'I must destroy the earth. I have decided to bring waters upon the earth. I have decided to let it rain.'"

At that, Noah would have said, "Oh, God, what is rain?"

Until that moment things had been wetted from a mist that came up from the earth. They did not know storm clouds. They did not know swirling rains that fall with rapidity and strength.

So God said, "Noah, water will come down from

heaven. Also, I will open the fountains of the deep. I will cover every high mountain with water."

Noah had to accept or not accept something that had never before happened.

God said, "Noah, I will send the water. You must build a boat. Take with you on the boat seven pairs of each of the clean animals and one pair of the unclean to preserve them. Bring your household into the ark. I have accepted your family—your wife, your sons, and your sons' wives. All other flesh upon the earth will be destroyed. I will preserve you, and you will be like unto Adam. From you will come all peoples that ever will walk upon the face of the earth."

What a tremendous thing. It was bigger than Noah could imagine.

He could have said, "Now, Lord, I'm a farmer. I know how to plow. I don't even know what an ark is. I've never seen the big waters You are talking about. All I know is that if I plow and plant, we have plenty to eat. We're getting along fine."

God said, "Now listen, Noah. Right down through the middle of this field, I want you to layout a diagram I will give you to build the boat."

Noah may have said, "Lord, I'm not a carpenter. I'm not a designer—especially of boats. Nevertheless, Lord, I will do as You ask."

Faith is a quality of the unknown. If you cannot move with God in the area of the unknown, you cannot demonstrate living, vital, pertinent faith before God. Noah demonstrated such faith to every succeeding generation.

> *Faith is a quality of the unknown. If you cannot move with God in the area of the unknown, you cannot demonstrate living, vital, pertinent faith before God.*

He probably talked it over with his family. And they joined with him to build the ark God designed.

Until 1850 no boat sailed the seas as large as Noah's ark. Today men who know say that the dimensions of the ark given in the Bible are the best dimensions for floating dead weight.

God told Noah how to build it, and Noah said, "I'm willing to work for You."

That touches me deeply. Millions of people work for themselves alone. But I can tell you from the depths of my heart that since I was a boy, I've never worked for myself. I've only worked for God.

At seventeen I became a minister and began to conduct meetings. To see souls saved I worked hard. I wouldn't take a day off. I'd finish on Sunday in one city and begin on Monday in another.

At twenty I became a missionary. I set off to go around the world with only $12. No denominations or churches supported me. God said, "Go," and I went.

You say, "How could you do that?"

Faith is the only answer we have for these things. Only faith can get it done. Faith is a labor, and I went off around the world laboring.

Sometimes I would ride on the backs of animals from daylight to dark. Then I'd eat some food and talk to the people in the towns we came to every night. My bones ached while I preached to them, "I've come to tell you the story." They would say, "We've never heard a story like this. But we're glad to hear it." Muscles ached. I was so tired. Yet I continued.

I've continued through the years until this very moment. How? You can only do it through one strength—faith. Faith is labor. Faith is working for God.

Some years ago when I gave up my church in South Bend, Indiana, to go to the mission field, I called five or six outstanding ministers and said, "Would you like to have a great church?"

They said, "We'll come look at it."

When they came, they saw the church. They saw the radio program. They saw the print shop and the program of printing literature. They saw the bookstore. They saw the day school. They saw the nursery. They saw the school for the blind.

Then they said, "We don't want the job."

The first thing two or three of them wanted to know was if there was time to play golf every morning and if they could have at least two days off a week.

"A day off?" I said. "I don't know what you mean by a day off. I labor every day of my life for Jesus." And I'm not a fool. I do it because the dividends are there. One day I'll cash those dividends when I see Jesus. And He will say, "You worked for Me."

Faith has to do with labor. I didn't say it—God

said it. God told Noah to build an ark, and He called the instrument that produced it faith.

Noah had no ability to do it, but he did it anyway. The powers of faith came into being, and he carried out the directions of the Holy Spirit as they were spoken to him. He obeyed and did the job.

You don't need a great amount of strength or ability to work for God. I read of a little lady who was an invalid. She wanted to work for Jesus, so she ordered tracts. She stamped on the back of them a few words telling where they could contact her if they needed more help. Then she sat by her window and waited for someone to walk by. She'd pray over a tract and drop it out the window. Letters began to come back. Souls began to get saved. Soon she was getting more souls saved than most preachers in the town. She was an invalid, but she didn't quit working.

Faith is an act. Faith is a work. Most people think faith is something like witchcraft: "You die." "You live." "You come down." "You go up." No! Faith is reality. Faith is living. Faith is a gift to God's work. Faith is a walk with God. Faith is a labor. Bunyons on your toes. Knees hard from kneeling and praying.

Martin Luther said, "It is a busy, active, living reality that does not ask, 'What shall I do?' But before the time that you ask, you're already up doing it. This is faith."

Faith has to do with looking for a work to do and getting it done.

David's job was to kill a giant. David was a youth. The giant was a monster. David knew he couldn't combat him physically. He had to find another way. He had to have faith for it.

Faith is an act. Faith is a work. God would cause the giant to fall. But David had to work with what he had.

God never asks for what you don't have. Some say, "Oh, God, if I had a million dollars, I'd give it to You." Don't tell God lies. Give Him what you've got, and He believes it. Don't cry, "Oh, God, if. . . ." Forget the word "if." There are no ifs, ands, or buts about it. We can do it, or we can't do it. We will do it, or we won't do it. Live in a world of dynamic reality. Start where you are with what you have.

David said, "I don't have a sword. I was offered one, but it didn't fit. But I do have a sling. Slings are not for warfare, but that's all I've got so I'll use it."

He took a smooth stone out of a brook, wound the sling, and threw it with all his might. Now that stone had to get past a lot of things. It first had to get past a man with a shield dancing up and down and sideways to keep anything from coming at Goliath. It had to get past Goliath's armor. God used His radar to direct the stone to an open place between the giant's eyes. Goliath was stunned. He fell to the ground. David ran and grabbed Goliath's sword and cut off his head. David manifested laboring faith.

That's the same kind of faith Noah had. And what a job he had to do. He had to lay down the timbers. They didn't have iron nails at the time, so he had to make some kind of nails or wooden plugs. We don't know how, but he began to put that thing together. He sweated. It was hard. He had callouses.

Not many people want to work for God. There are many who dream of it, but they're actually too lazy to do it. People talk about doing personal evangelism— going person to person and talking about Jesus—but it's only a dream. They are too lazy to do it. They say, "Maybe I don't have faith." Faith is an act. Faith has to do with labor. If they had faith, it would demonstrate itself in labor.

I have lived in a hundred nations. I have preached in a thousand cities. But I have not found many people who really want to work for God. If they work, it's always for temporal purposes—to make money, etc. It is not to do something for God. It is not a labor of love—a labor because of intense love for God. Yet God calls that faith.

Are you still with me? Don't lay down this book now. Don't be like some who have heard me teach on faith. They begin to pray, "Lord, I was only joking. I don't really want faith." When they come to the very essence of it and find faith is a sacrifice, they back off and say, "I don't want to make a sacrifice." When they find faith is walking with God and has nothing to do with living a voluptuous life of the world, they say, "I want my freedoms." They don't want to live close to God in prayer, in communion, in reading the Word, in blessing other people. They say, "We want faith, but we don't want to live close to God." They **cannot** have faith. Then when it comes to the sweat, they say,

"Wait a minute, I don't think I want that kind of thing."

Are you willing to subject yourself to labor for Jesus?

Then rise up and say, "I am ready now to be sacrificial toward You, God. I am ready to walk with You, God. I am ready to work with You, God. Oh, God, put a desire for working within me that I will be like Noah, that I will build Your Kingdom on the face of this earth. I dedicate my own brawn and strength to You, in Jesus' name."

That is faith!

14
Faith Is a Pilgrimage

By faith Abraham, when he was called to go out into a place which he should after receive for an inheritance, obeyed; and he went out, not knowing whither he went.

By faith he sojourned in the land of promise, as in a strange country, dwelling in tabernacles with Isaac and Jacob, the heirs with him of the same promise:

For he looked for a city which hath foundations, whose builder and maker is God (Hebrews 11:8-11).

We have come now to one I really love: Faith is a pilgrimage.

If we could call Abraham down from heaven (he won't come), we would say, "Abraham, we're excited about faith. God spoke highly of your faith. Tell us what faith is."

Abraham probably could not tell us the secret of his greatness because with him faith was a life, not a definition. He would only say something like this: "I was living in a big beautiful home in a culturally advanced city. I held a place of prominence in the area. I had flocks and much pasture land around the city.

The great Euphrates flowed down in front of us, and we had lots of water. We seemingly had all we needed. But God spoke to me and said, 'Separate yourself from this people. Separate yourself from this sinful worshiping of idols and the devil.'

"Then He said, 'Separate yourself from this beautiful home. I want you to live in a tent the rest of your life. Never again will you live in a house.' (Isn't that beautiful! Live in a tent the rest of your life!)

"But God also said, 'I am going to make you a great person. I am going to give you a country. I want you to go to that country now.'"

I can hear Abraham say, "Well, Lord, very interesting. Do You have a map?"

The Lord said, "No, I don't give maps. Every day I will guide you for that day. I will bring you into that country where you shall live. And, Abraham, I will whisper this to you: "I have a city not made with human hands. One day you can live in that city."

So Abraham left looking for a city which has foundations whose builder and maker is God. Abraham knew about the New Jerusalem! Isn't that amazing!

Abraham left a city looking for a city.

"Oh," you say, "the city he left was only a primitive town."

Wrong. It was a very great city. The Museum of Natural History in London has on display relics of the early Chaldees. There I have seen the beautiful gold filigree work of their artisans. I have seen sections of their intricate below-street-level sewage system.

"Sewage system? In that day?" Yes!

They had cobblestone streets. It was not a second-rate town. It was not a village. It was a city of comfort, beauty, and riches.

God said, "Abraham, give it up. Give up your friends. Give up the philosophers you talk with. Give up the whole thing, Abraham, and follow Me."

Abraham did it! Faith is a pilgrimage.

You can't tell how strong someone is by his surroundings. He might die for his job. He wouldn't give it up for anything. They pay him to work on the Lord's day and he obeys. He may be bound to his home. He'd die for that house he built. He loves it above everything. Such a one is not a pilgrim. He is very well settled.

God may never want you to give up everything. But He wants you *willing* to do it. He wants you to say from your heart, "Lord, I am willing to do it."

There are people who say, "Brother Sumrall, I'm supposed to preach. God told me to."

I say, "Why don't you preach?"

"Well, I haven't gotten into it."

Then usually I know, and I say, "God doesn't want you to preach. God wants you *willing* to preach. After you say, 'Lord, I'm willing,' He wants you to go ahead and do your work. But you must be willing. You must not be a rebel. You must not say, 'Nothing doing.'"

God wanted Abraham to go into action. His faith was demonstrated by a pilgrimage. He gave up his friends. He gave up his land and his home. He gave up everything. He walked out of Ur of the Chaldees looking for a city that had foundations whose builder and maker was God. And God called it faith.

Several years ago I sat at a table in a big restaurant with a minister and his wife. I'm a missionary. I've always been a missionary. I've lived in over a hundred nations. I've preached around this world many times. My heart is missions. Missions flow through me all the time. So I was talking to them about missions.

The man looked at me and said, "Brother Sumrall, God has called me to India. God told me that if I will go to a certain city in India (and he named it), He will give me a great move of the Spirit of God and hundreds, even thousands, will be saved. Oh, I want to go so badly I don't know what to do."

I didn't know it, but he was telling me this because of his wife. I soon learned it, however, because she suddenly burst out crying. Then she began to talk. Her face got red in anger.

"If you want to go to India, go by yourself!"

I looked at him. I looked at her.

I've got the nicest wife in the world. She'd go to the moon with me if I'd provide two tickets. Anywhere I've asked her to go, she was always ready. The Philippines. Hong Kong. We lived in Israel during a war. I had to say, "Honey, the American government will give us free tickets out of here to go home. Do you want them?" She said, "No, I'll stay with you. We'll go through the war together." She wasn't afraid. When we went to the Philippines, the war in Korea was red hot and burning. I said, "Honey, it's a flaming war. Do you want to go?" She said, "Let's go." I have a wonderful wife. She's part of me. She flows with me. All I have to say is, "Let's do it," and she says, "Let's do it now."

I thank God for a wife like her. Perhaps that's why I was so shocked at this woman's outburst. She cried, "I will not go to India. I will not live with those dirty, filthy people. I will not be without my refrigerator. I will not be without my conveniences here in my home. I will not. I will die before I will go."

Her husband began to comfort her, "Now, darling."

I have watched that minister from that day to this. And I have not seen many smiles on his face. He has suffered defeats in many areas of life. He wasn't a pilgrim.

I want to tell you something. If Sarah had wanted to stay in Ur of the Chaldees, she never would have seen Abraham's face again. Abraham was leaving. If she had not wanted to go, she could have stayed there and died there. Abraham might have left her his house, too. He was a rich man. But Abraham was going to obey God.

Faith is a personal affair. You have it. Your spouse has it. Your children have it. If you are head of the house, your faith should flow out to the whole family. But faith is an individual thing. I can't have faith for you. You can't have faith for me. We must each have our own living, glorious, marvelous, wonderful faith. Abraham didn't have all the faith in his house. Sarah left all, too.

> *I can't have faith for you. You can't have faith for me. We must each have our own living, glorious, marvelous, wonderful faith.*

Faith is an act. Abraham loaded his camels and donkeys with goods. His wagons came out of there and started north up the river. He rode out of the city and said, "Good-bye." He cut communication with that land. He became a pilgrim.

A Pilgrim Spirit

You can have a pilgrim spirit without physically leaving everything. Abraham had a pilgrim spirit. He didn't love the things of the world. He loved God. We must all have that pilgrim spirit. "Lord, I'll go where You want me to go. I'll do what You want me to do." That is the spirit of a pilgrim that flows through us and says, "Lord, I've cut all the ropes. What do You want?"

God spoke to me at three o'clock one afternoon and said, "Go live in Manila, Philippines, for Me."

I said, "Lord, I've been to Manila. Ninety percent of it is in ruins. I've seen rats as big as cats there. Lord, do You want me and my family to go live in that place?"

God said, "I certainly do. And I'll do more for you there than ever before."

I prayed a little longer in my room. God spoke to me three times and said the same thing. I walked downstairs where my wife was cooking dinner.

I said, "Honey, we're going to Manila."

She had never before heard a word about it. She looked into my eyes and dropped her cooking spoon. Tears came to her eyes. She said, "When are we going?"

I said, "Tonight."

"Oh," she said, "we can't go tonight."

I said, "Yes."

That night I called in the deacons of the church and resigned. I said, "I'm going." And I put into action the whole force.

I left my home. I left my church. You may think it's hard to leave a home. You ought to have to leave a church of a thousand people—many of whom you brought to Jesus, all of whom are yours. Just to walk off and leave them. You don't know pain. You don't know sorrow. But when God says do it, you do it. Within a few days, I'd placed them with a pastor. And I'd taken off for Manila to work for God.

There's where He did the miracle for me. In two years we had seven to eight thousand coming to church on Sunday. In two years the whole nation had heard I was there. The power of God had come and done great wonders in the nation. In one revival meeting one hundred and fifty thousand came to Jesus.

Why would He do all those things? I was His pilgrim. I didn't love my home in South Bend. I didn't
love my church building in South Bend. I said, "Lord,
it's Yours."

That is faith. I didn't realize it was faith when I did
it. God told me that later. I just thought it was obeying God. But that is faith. Faith is a pilgrimage.

Are you ready to cut anything God will have you
cut? To become a pilgrim? To walk with God and say,
"Lord, I'm not married to the things of this world"?

If God were to ask me to leave our television sta-
tions, our radio station, our great church, our international headquarters, and all the ministry we have, I
wouldn't lose one night's rest. I'd say, "Praise God!
Now we've got something big to do. Let's get going
now, Lord." My faith in God is such that anything He
removes I accept as His will. He'd just get that out of
the way to provide something bigger.

Yet some are so afraid of their jobs. They're so
afraid of their houses. They're so afraid of the mun-
dane things around them until they're married to them.
And they don't have faith.

Faith is a pilgrimage. Are you willing to go with
God? Abraham did.

Can you see his grim face that morning when
with a big stick in his hand he went plowing out of
the city?

Can you hear the inhabitants laughing, "Oh, there
goes a fool! We won't ever hear from you anymore!"

As it turned out, no one hears of them anymore.

Nothing but a sand dune is there now. But Abraham! The whole world has heard of Abraham!

Imagine a man with such capacity that at the voice of God he cut everything loose. To him, he was walking into oblivion. There were no guarantees. Nothing was out there but God. So He walked and talked with God in faith.

Sometimes through disaster or persecution people lose houses and businesses. What would *you* do? Commit suicide? Or would you be joyful and rejoice in the Lord? In some countries people lose their jobs because they don't go along with the government's atheistic stand. What would *you* do?

Faith is a pilgrimage with God—just breaking loose from everything and saying, "Lord, have Your way. I'm walking with You."

What a glorious life it is! What a thrilling, magnificent situation you can have within your heart! Faith is the most wonderful thing. Faith could change this world if we had men and women who would pay the price for having it.

Too many say, "We don't want any. Number one: We don't want to give to God. Number two: We don't want to walk with God. Number three: We don't want to work for God. And for God's sake, we don't want to be a pilgrim! We want to get anchored down. We want security."

The world is being destroyed by what people call security.

My strength is in God. My security is in God.

I depend on no one but Jesus Christ. I am tied to nothing but Jesus Christ.

> *Faith is a pilgrimage. I depend on no one but Jesus Christ.*

15
Faith Is a Woman's Courage

Through faith also Sara herself received
strength to conceive seed, and was delivered
of a child when she was past age, because
she judged him faithful who had promised.
   Therefore sprang there even of one, and
him as good as dead, so many as the stars of
the sky in multitude, and as the sand which
is by the sea shore innumerable (Hebrews
11:11, 12).

There are, and there have been, many great
women of faith. Some of these women have touched
my own life. My mother blessed my life. She taught
me about God. She lived a life that made me want to
discover God.

Women of faith have performed monumental
works of blessing and glory, especially on the mission fields of the world. There was a time when there
were at least three women missionaries on the field
to one male missionary. At home, women of faith have
risen up like towers of strength to bless the Church.
They are real. They challenge the devil.

The Bible says that faith gave Sarah strength to conceive a son named Isaac. Her husband, Abraham,

was one hundred years old when Isaac was born (Genesis 21:5). Sarah was ninety. Ishmael, the half-Egyptian boy brought into the scene by Hagar the maidservant, was fourteen. With these numbers in mind, we see how persistent Sarah's faith was.

Some pray for something three minutes and when they don't get it, they say, "Shucks!" That's all they get, too.

Sarah didn't operate in hope. Hope has no foundations that will persist. Hope can be blinded. Hope can be hurt. Hope can be placed into an embarrassing position where it says, "Well, I was only hoping for it anyway."

But faith is a strength, a tower, a fort. Faith is an impregnable mountain that will not move. Faith persists; it has staying power.

> *Faith is a strength, a tower, a fort.*
> *Faith is an impregnable mountain*
> *that will not move.*

It may be that with the other people we have talked about their aspect of faith was easier. Enoch walked with God. That wasn't bad. Abel gave an excellent sacrifice. That wasn't too hard. You give what you see and feel. Sarah accepted faith as living fact. That's what made her famous. The Bible says that through this thing called faith she accepted a promise as a fact.

The key word to Sarah's faith is "because." The Bible says,

> *. . . because she judged him* [God] *faithful who had promised.*
> *Therefore sprang there even of one, and him as good as dead, so many as the stars of the sky in multitude, and as the sand which is by the sea shore innumerable* (Hebrews 11:11, 12).

If we could speak to her and ask, "Sarah, God said you had faith. What is faith?" she would reply, "Since God said it, that is the final word on the subject."

Sarah judged God to be faithful as He had promised.

We consult our neighbors. We consult our relatives. "What do you think?" we ask them. If they're not spiritual, they think a lot of foolish things. Sometimes those who are spiritual don't have a relationship of faith as you have, so they think you are foolish.

The Bible does not say Abraham had the faith for this boy. It says Sarah did. She would tell us the secret of her faith when she said, "Because I judged Him faithful Who had promised."

When God makes a promise to you, me, or anybody, He will fulfill that promise. When God says He will do something, He doesn't want us to cringe and say, "Well, maybe." There are no maybe's with God.

Why Sarah Had to Believe

After the Fall in the Garden of Eden, God gave the first remarkable promise of man's redemption: *And I will put enmity between thee* [Lucifer] *and the woman, and between thy seed and her seed; it shall bruise thy head, and thou shalt bruise his heel* (Genesis 3:15).

The seed of woman would break Satan's lordship.

From that moment Satan sought to stop it from happening. He didn't know how long it would take. Every time he saw something developing, he attempted to stop it. That's why Cain killed Abel. It wasn't that they were so angry with each other. It was that the devil moved in and said, "If I can have one of them kill the other, the one left is a murderer. They won't bruise my head."

Years later God said to Abraham, *I will make of thee a great nation . . . and in thee shall all families of the earth be blessed* (Genesis 12:2, 3). Through Abraham God would bring a Redeemer for the whole world.

The devil thought, *I've got to stop that.* And I believe he closed the womb of this woman. This was a diabolical thing. Sarah wasn't just fighting nature—she was fighting all the forces of hell.

You may be doing the same thing and are unaware of it. That's where we fail. We think we're fighting natural things. If you want something from God and you're not getting it, start resisting the devil. Don't start fighting your family.

> **If you want something from God and you're not getting it, start resisting the devil. Don't start fighting your family.**

For seventy years Sarah waited. She was married seventy years with no child. After five years people began to talk: "What's the matter, Sarah? Everybody is having babies but you. You must be a really sinful person."

If something goes wrong, that's the first thing the devil throws at you, "You're not living right." He's a liar. He knows you're living right.

Women holding their own babies may have said to Sarah, "God doesn't care much for you." Yes, God cared a lot for her.

Just because the devil is persecuting you does not mean God doesn't love you.

I think I know what Sarah did during the time she waited. If she hadn't done it, she never would have had the child. I think every morning when she got up she took her pillow, put it in her arms, hugged it tightly, and said, "Good morning, darling. How are you, my son?" Then she danced all over her tent singing a lullaby to her baby.

Her maids, Hagar especially, laughed, "Ha! Ha! Ha! Our mistress is getting ready. She's getting gray hair and wrinkles. But she's getting no babies. After all, there are laws of nature."

Who said God has to work with the laws of nature? He made them. He could reverse them right now if He wanted to and everything would work opposite to what it's been working. Wouldn't that mess up things for a while? God is no servant to the laws of nature. And neither are we.

Every morning as Sarah danced around the tent,

Faith Can Change Your World

she said: "I'm going to have him. It doesn't matter if I'm forty and the way of women is ceasing. . . It doesn't matter if I'm fifty and it's been gone for ten years. . . It doesn't matter if I'm sixty. . . seventy. . . eighty. . . I'll have him at ninety!"

Faith holds on, and Sarah was holding. She held tightly to the last moment when it all began to happen.

I can tell you what the others said after they saw her stomach growing. They said, "She's too old to have a baby. She'll die in childbirth."

Don't listen to the devil. He'll try to keep you in more trouble than you can imagine. With him, *nothing* works. With us, *everything* works. Glory be to God, we make it work!

Quitters don't make anything work. People who become discouraged show they have lost their source of faith. If you let your source of faith dry up, there's no blessing. Our source of faith is to involve ourselves as Sarah did in the promises of God. I can get completely hilarious just by reading the promises of God. "Whewie! Just look at all I've got here!"

> ***Our source of faith is to involve ourselves as Sarah did in the promises of God.***

Sarah's source of strength was demonstrated in her confession, "I believe Him to be faithful Who has promised. I accept what He said." She walked on the promises of God.

142

Most people walk on their feelings. "Oh, yes, Brother Sumrall said I was healed, **but**. . . ." They're not healed now. That little three-letter word took care of everything. They're full of unbelief and doubt. "But I don't feel healed." They're in the soul. They've missed the place of faith—the spirit—and they're in their soulical parts.

Sarah could have died without a child. God could have found another woman. He could have found another man. No human is indispensable to God. But when you've got faith and the devil is attacking you, hang in there. God will be with you. Just hang in there! When it looks the worst, that's when it's getting better. When it seems as though it won't work, that's when it's already working. That's what faith is all about.

Natural-minded people never have understood people of faith. When Sarah acted every day as though she had a son and talked about it, saying, "I will have a son," not one woman in the whole area believed it. They all said, "All history is against you. All experience is against you. All knowledge is against you." That's where faith begins—at the end of that business.

Sarah had to have said, "I am resting on the promise of God." Catch the word *resting*. Some are *irritated* on the promises of God, but faith rests. The Bible says, *For we which have believed do enter into rest* . . . (Hebrews 4:3). One in faith says, "I am resting on the promises of God. I've learned to sleep during the storm. Let the waves rage. Let the winds blow. There is sleep."

> ***For we which have believed do enter into rest . . . (Hebrews 4:3).***

Until you can learn to rest in the promises of God, they are not valid to you. If your insides burn and roll in turmoil, these promises will not be for you. You have to know that God keeps His promises, and you have to rest in them. That's what Sarah did. She was not tormented. She rejoiced in the promises of God. That's the way you get them.

Sarah was no nervous wreck. She didn't come out in the morning with her hair going four dozen ways, saying, "Oh, my God! My God!" When she came out, she looked like a princess—that was her name. At seventy-five she was so pretty they thought she was a girl.

This woman knew God would move the constellations before He would fail her. She knew God would make it come to pass. She stands as a Gibraltar of fidelity and faith.

We look not only to her, but to her daughters after her: Jochebed, the mother of Moses; Miriam, the amazing sister of Moses; Esther, the queen of an empire; and Mary, the mother of Jesus. If you knew Mary a little better, Mary might say, "If God can do it for my great-grandmother, Sarah, He can do it for me.

If she was a hundred years old and conceived, then I can conceive by the power of the Holy Ghost."

That faith did not remain just in Sarah's bosom; it flowed down through centuries. We trust that today it is in all our hearts and that we will see a woman change the world by believing the promises of God.

Sarah's faith was believing and accepting the promises of God. The promises of God are sure. Let's believe them. Let's accept them. Let's live by them. They are not just for the ladies. They're for everybody. And as we do what Sarah did, the same God Who answered her prayers will answer ours.

16
Faith Is a Choice

By faith Moses, when he was born, was hid three months of his parents, because they saw he was a proper child; and they were not afraid of the king's commandment.

By faith Moses, when he was come to years, refused to be called the son of Pharaoh's daughter;

Choosing rather to suffer affliction with the people of God, than to enjoy the pleasures of sin for a season;

Esteeming the reproach of Christ greater riches than the treasures in Egypt: for he had respect unto the recompence of the reward.

By faith he forsook Egypt, not fearing the wrath of the king: for he endured, as seeing him who is invisible.

Through faith he kept the passover, and the sprinkling of blood, lest he that destroyed the firstborn should touch them.

By faith they passed through the Red sea as by dry land: which the Egyptians assaying to do were drowned (Hebrews 11:23-29).

Moses' parents *decided* to go against the king's

command. They were not afraid. God called their *decision* faith.

Such people are mission builders. They are city builders. They are not afraid of a shadow. Thank God for courage. Thank God for people who know what they believe and believe it with all their hearts. It's no shame to go to jail for the right thing. Some of the greatest men in history lived in jail. It's a shame to do wrong. It's no shame to do right, no matter how you are persecuted.

> *Thank God for courage. Thank God for people who know what they believe and believe it with all their hearts.*

Moses *chose* to suffer affliction with the people of God rather than to enjoy the pleasures of sin for a season, esteeming the reproach of Christ greater riches than the treasures of Egypt. And God called Moses' *choice* faith.

Faith is a *decision.*

Faith is a *choice.*

Moses' parents made a decision. The wicked king of Egypt said, "Every Israelite boy baby must die." Jochebed, the mother of Moses, said, "That's all *you* know. I've got other designs for my son."

Jochebed said, "I'll give my baby to the queen, and let her rear him for me." She must have prayed, "God, I'm going to put him in a basket in the river right where the princess comes to bathe. Lord, I want him to be reared in the palace, not killed in the gutter."

What a woman! We need mothers like that today. That's faith. That's decision. That's choice. That's making history. That's not living by the whims of society. That's making society. The man she produced changed the world.

She had faith in her heart. She took her little baby, wrapped him up, put him in a basket in the Nile River, and shoved him over to where the princess bathed. She put her daughter, Miriam, to watch over the infant with these orders, "When the princess finds him, only say, 'Who do you want to take care of him?' Then come get me, honey."

Talk about faith! Faith is a decision.

What kind of decisions are you making? Decisions of doubt? Decisions of confusion? Are you crying, "Oh, what's going to happen to me tomorrow?" If you are, you don't have faith.

I'm not afraid of tomorrow. I'm not afraid of communism. I'm not afraid of revolution. I'm not afraid of anything. I'm making the decisions for tomorrow myself. You've got to do the same thing. That's faith—living, dynamic faith; faith that changes the world!

Moses' family lived faith. They had the real thing. You know the story. The princess found the babe. Little Miriam came running up and said, "Don't you want a nurse to take care of this little one? I can find one for you."

The princess said, "Well, yes. He's so pretty."

Miriam brought her mother and said, "This lady will take care of him real cheap."

Imagine getting paid to take care of your own child. That's decision for you.

But the big decisions came from Moses. He lived forty years in the palace. He knew all the wisdom of Egypt at its highest peak of empire. When Egypt was at its richest, highest, and greatest, Moses rose up in the palace. He played around the throne. He kissed the princess. The pharaoh embraced him and loved him.

It must have angered the devil to see how Jochebed had said, "It's got to be," and how she pushed it by her faith. Things happened then because of faith, and they happen now by faith.

Moses stayed in the palace until he was forty, then that spirit of his mother got into him and said, "All right, you've had enough of intellectualism. You've had enough of riches. It's time now to get into My business. Let's get going and deliver the people out of this bondage."

At forty years of age, when it was time for him to sit on the throne, Moses stood before the whole kingdom and said, "I am not a pharaoh. I am not the son of the pharaoh's daughter. I am a Hebrew. I will suffer with my people. I refuse to sit upon that golden throne with a golden scepter and rule this rich and flourishing empire. I will live with the slaves."

Would you have done that? Think twice. Don't lie to yourself. Would you give up your job for Jesus' sake? Would you give up your house for Jesus' sake? Would you give up your relatives for Jesus' sake?

This man had something. He was to sit on the throne and be Pharaoh III, or something like that. But that's all he would ever have been. He could have enjoyed his riches and died. But he didn't. He became immortalized.

The Bible says he did it through this instrument of faith we've been talking about. It wasn't anything else. God said faith did it, so that means faith is a decision. It's a choice you make.

Moses said, "I refuse to be called the son of Pharaoh's daughter. I choose to accept my people in their bondage and slavery." He chose to take off his royal garments and to put on the slave's garment.

He mistakenly thought he could help his people in his own strength, however. He thought he could use the wisdom and strength of Egypt. He thought perhaps he could lure out half the army on his side.

God said, "That's not the way." God had to send him to the desert for forty years to get Moses out of Moses. God can get you out of Egypt (a type of sin) quicker than he can get Egypt out of you. You can get saved quickly. But God has a hard time getting some of the rotten stuff out of you that somebody else put in. It took God a few minutes to an hour to get Moses out of the country, but it took Him forty years to get Egypt out of Moses.

When God got it all out, He sent Moses back as a mighty man. But this time with no swords, just a staff in his hand. This time Moses had God's power, not man's power. This time he was making decisions of faith to save God's people and to affect the world.

I have a little saying: "You make a decision; the decision makes you."

Some make negative decisions, and they are negative people. Make positive decisions and be a positive person.

You can see it in natural life. Henry Ford had a conviction that automobiles could be mass produced. Nobody else had that conviction. They said that a man had to make every piece of an automobile and put them together by hand. They said only the wealthy could ever afford one. But Ford said, "None of this! Put it on the line. Let every man screw a screw and make it cheap." Before he died, even the janitor cleaning the floor had an automobile, and Ford left over a billion dollars behind. It was because of a decision he made.

Frank Winfield Woolworth was a small town merchant. But he had a conviction within him: stock a whole store with five-and-ten-cent goods; then through the selling of masses of it, you'd get rich. It worked. He had to forget the kind of store he had and say, "I'm going to build stores like this throughout the world." When he died, Mr. Woolworth left over sixty million dollars for his family. He made a decision, then the decision made him.

Oh, if we could get Christians to make decisions of faith! The Bible declares that the just shall live by faith. Our existence is to be by faith.

> **The Bible declares that the just shall live by faith. Our existence is to be by faith.**

I don't know how spiritual Ford and Woolworth were, but they each made a decision. They made a choice. They made a good one, and it worked.

If you can come to that, you will never again be the same. Most of us have great opportunities in our lives. If we say no to them, we lose them. If we accept them and the challenge that goes with them, we can change the world.

Look what Moses did. He led more than two million out of Egypt to Mount Sinai and God. He received the Law upon which every nation that has good law today bases its law. Nothing man ever has conceived in the history of the world can beat the Ten Commandments. The Mosaic Law incorporates a judicial system and a family system.

Moses' mother made a decision. Moses made a decision of faith. Faith is a decision. Are you ready to make some decisions? Are you ready to make a choice and stick by it? A positive choice? A God choice? Then that is faith!

17

Faith on a String

By faith the harlot Rahab perished not with them that believed not, when she had received the spies with peace (Hebrews 11:31).

Now this is a most audacious scripture. Imagine naming a harlot right after Moses in this passage! Imagine putting a harlot with Abraham and Sarah, then classifying her as having the same faith, the same force, and the same power! A harlot somehow slipped into this great gallery of heroes. Her picture is up there on the wall alongside Enoch and all the marvelous people of Hebrews, chapter 11.

How did she make it? God said it was **by faith.**

I'm glad to get to this chapter because now you will believe that you can have it. It doesn't matter how far down you've gone. God can bring you up into the celebrity group and make you one of the great faith heroes of our time. If a harlot can make it, *you* can. It doesn't matter if you've been in jail, on drugs, sold your body for sin, or whatever. If you will come to God and believe Him, your name can be enrolled in the gallery of faith heroes with the beautiful memorial under your picture: Here is a person of faith.

> ***If you will come to God and believe Him, your name can be enrolled in the gallery of faith heroes.***

By faith the harlot Rahab. . . . The Bible is a candid book. It calls a spade a spade. It calls a harlot a harlot. Jesus said He cast seven devils out of Mary Magdalene. Until the day she died, she was Mary Magdalene out of whom were cast seven devils. The Bible is a book of truth. How glad we are for the truth!

By faith the harlot Rahab perished not with them that believed not. . . . It wasn't that Rahab was any better than anybody else in Jericho. No doubt there were people in that city a thousand degrees better than she was. But she became the person she became because she believed. Her whole city mocked God and worshiped images. She wouldn't do it. She believed. She was different from everybody else in town. Because of it, her house stood when every other house fell.

Would your home stand when every other house in town went to pieces? What kind of home are you building? Rahab built hers on faith. The Bible says she did it by faith—not with brains, not with money. She believed something.

I call this chapter "Faith on a String" because of the string Rahab put outside the window to identify her house. It was a red string. Some have said it typifies the blood of the Lord Jesus Christ.

By her faith she perished not with them that believed not. You don't have to die with this generation. You don't have to go to hell with this generation. You don't have to suffer the diseases of this generation because the Bible says, . . . *by whose stripes ye were healed* (1 Peter 2:24).

Oh, you'll have to have faith. You'll have to resist. You'll have to fight. But you will win. Faith is a wonderful thing.

Rahab perished not with them that believed not. They just would not believe. If they had believed, they'd have opened their doors and let in the people of Israel, saying: "Come in. We welcome you. We give up our gods. We serve no other God but Jehovah. We become your servants." Immediately the whole city would have changed. There would have been no falling of the walls of Jericho. But they would not do it. They trusted in themselves. They trusted in idols. They blasphemed Jehovah. When Israel walked around the walls six days, the people laughed at them and said they were crazy. But they soon found out they were not crazy. On the seventh day the walls fell!

Only one person had sense to see it—Rahab.

Justified by Works

Rahab perished not with them that believed not, when she had received the spies with peace. James 2:25 says, *Likewise also was not Rahab the harlot justified by works, when she had received the messengers, and had sent them out another way?*

Rahab was justified by her actions of faith. What were they? Let's look back at some excerpts from the Old Testament account:

And Joshua the son of Nun sent out of Shittim two men to spy secretly, saying, Go view the land, even Jericho. And they went, and came into an harlot's house, named Rahab, and lodged there. . .

And the king of Jericho sent unto Rahab, saying, Bring forth the men that are come to thee, which are entered into thine house: for they be come to search out all the country.

And the woman took the two men, and hid them, and said thus, There came men unto me, but I wist not whence they were . . .

But she had brought them up to the roof of the house, and hid them with the stalks of flax, which she had laid in order upon the roof. . .

And before they were laid down, she came up unto them upon the roof;

And she said unto the men, I know that the LORD hath given you the land, and that your terror is fallen upon us, and that all the inhabitants of the land faint because of you.

For we have heard how the LORD dried up the water of the Red sea for you, when ye came out of Egypt; and what ye did unto the two kings of the Amorites, that were on the other side Jordan, Sihon and Og, whom ye utterly destroyed.

And as soon as we had heard these things,

our hearts did melt, neither did there remain any more courage in any man, because of you: for the LORD your God, he is God in heaven above, and in earth beneath.

Now therefore, I pray you, swear unto me by the LORD, since I have shewed you kindness, that ye will also shew kindness unto my father's house, and give me a true token:

And that ye will save alive my father, and my mother, and my brethren, and my sisters, and all that they have, and deliver our lives from death.

And the men answered her, Our life for yours, if ye utter not this our business. And it shall be, when the LORD hath given us the land, that we will deal kindly and truly with thee.

Then she let them down by a cord through the window: for her house was upon the town wall, and she dwelt upon the wall.

And she said unto them, Get you to the mountain, lest the pursuers meet you; and hide yourselves there three days, until the pursuers be returned: and afterward may ye go your way.

And the men said unto her, We will be blameless of this thine oath which thou hast made us swear.

Behold, when we come into the land, thou shalt bind this line of scarlet thread in the window which thou didst let us down by: and thou shalt bring thy father, and thy mother, and thy brethren, and all thy father's household, home unto thee (Joshua 2:1, 3, 4, 6, 8-18).

Rahab's faith had corresponding actions. She looked for the two spies and said, "Come into my house. You won't be safe anywhere else." When they came looking for them, she hid them in the flax on top of her house.

She must have been industrious. Flax is what they made cloth and many other things from in those days.

She must have been clever to have had a house on the wall. She had the fresh air. She could look out over the plains. It was a place of prestige.

She must have been strong. She let them down over the wall.

She knew how to do things—she wasn't stupid. She told the men how to save themselves and then to save her and her house. The men of Israel followed her advice.

She was a woman of faith. She knew God would give them the city. She made up her own mind. She decided to believe in the God of Israel when no one else in her culture did.

So it was by these works of hers that she was saved. Faith is an act. Faith is works. Faith is not dead; it is a living, working thing. You have to know that, or you can never have faith.

> *Faith is an act. Faith is works. Faith is not dead; it is a living, working thing.*

Her entire family was sheltered under the shadow of her faith. If you can have faith, it will be a shelter to your whole house.

Faith is a power. Faith is an anointing. Faith is a light. Faith is a strength. Faith is not an idea. Faith is not an abstraction. Faith is real. You can have more faith by faith acts—by faith doing.

Joshua and the children of Israel burned the city with fire after the walls fell, but not before they had brought out Rahab's entire house.

What a tremendous thing it was that she went in and became a part of the people of God, a part of the house of God. In fact, she became part of the very lineage of the Messiah. She is listed in Matthew, chapter 1, in the lineage of David. When she got into Israel, she married right. She didn't marry some stupid little idiot. She got into a good family. She was a good woman. She lived right.

When you come to Jesus, He forgives the past. Your neighbors may scar you forever, but God won't. When you come and show yourself to have faith in God, He forgives and eliminates the past. He casts it into the sea of His forgetfulness and never remembers your past again. He puts up a little sign: DEVIL, NO FISHING HERE. You're free forever. You don't have to bear the scarlet of the past. You can bear the righteousness of God—the white righteousness of His robes about you, cleanliness, holiness, and purity that come by living faith in the living God.

> **When you come and show yourself to have faith in God, He forgives and eliminates the past.**

Out of the fallen city of Jericho, one family rose up strong. They didn't come out as slaves. They didn't come out downtrodden. When they walked out of there, they said, "We helped deliver this city into your hands. Now we come to you to believe in your God and to serve Him and be a part of you."

Rahab got with the right kind of people. She came right into the family of the Messiah. And the Bible says it all happened by faith.

Where did she get her faith?

According to her words, she said, "We heard how you have been delivered from Egypt." That happened forty years before, but she heard the story and believed it.

She was strong minded. She knew what she wanted, and she went after it with all her might. She made up her mind. She said: "I believe these stories. I like this God that is with the people of Israel. I don't know Him, but I'm going to know Him someday. I have heard of all the things God did since you came out of Egypt until this day, and I believe God will deliver this land unto you."

That is faith. She heard and she believed.

Do you believe what you hear? Or do you say, "I don't believe that."

When I tell about Clarita Villanueva, the girl who was delivered from the devil's power in the Philippines, some say, "I don't know about that story."

I'm a funny fellow. I don't ask people to believe anything. They can believe if they want to—but I have to tell it because it is true. And I don't say, "Now, do you believe?" I leave it with them.

Rahab believed. Then she put her belief into action. She began to do something. When these men came, she accepted strangers. She said, "I accept you. I believe in you." She said, "I'll put my life on the line. If they find me, they'll kill me. I'll be dead and you will, too. But they won't find us. I'm too clever for them. I'll secure you. I'll hide you under the flax on top of my roof."

You say, "But she lied."

Yes. She was not a godly woman at that time. She was to move into that once she was delivered. Once she moved into the people of God, she would be taught the Ten Commandments. She would be taught things that are right, and she would do them from that time. Right then, however, she only knew what she wanted to be. She knew the church she wanted to join. She knew the group she wanted to be with, and she found a way to get in there. So she preserved these men. She let them go over the wall. She let them go free. She said, "I let you go free for one thing—save me that we can be a part of you."

She became a greater part than she'd ever dreamed. Maybe she thought she'd never be more than a servant, but God's too good for that. God saw the faith and courage that were in her. God said, "I'll do great things for you. You're the kind of person who pleases Me, a person who believes in Me. I count that for faith." So He included her in the beautiful story He wrote on faith in Hebrews, chapter 11.

We might downgrade her. We might spit upon her, but not God. God can do things men cannot do.

I preached in Alaska just before World War II. I met the mayor of the city and his wife. Someone told me their story (There are always gossipers around).

The mayor was a bachelor. He made a lot of money with gold, then got into politics and became mayor. There were few women there then. The men went down into the red light district. The mayor did, too. He found a girl there that he really liked.

He said, "Honey, do you want to be a harlot?"

She said, "No, but I have to make a living."

"Would you like to get out of here?"

"Yes."

"If I were to make you my wife, would you be a good woman?"

"Yes."

He took a girl out of the red light district and made her "Mrs. Mayor." When I met her, she was the most gracious person. Behind her back, others said, "Oh, she came out of the red light district," but to her face in government functions, she was Mrs. Mayor. She was first lady, and they had to admit it and accept it. She rose up out of her condition.

Anyone can. Faith can bring you out when nothing else can. By faith Rahab the harlot married into the lineage of David and Solomon and the Messiah Jesus.

Won't you rise up and believe God?

Faith is one of the vital issues of life. If you have it, you go places, you get things, you do things that never could have been done without the great flowing power of faith.

> **If you have faith, you go places, you get things, you do things that never could have been done without it. . . .**

Faith is of God. You get it from God, and it flows through you. It can bring you from the lowest to the highest. It can do things for you that you could never do in your own brawn or brain. You do them through the strength of the greatest force in the world—faith.

Jesus said, *All things are possible to him that believeth* (Mark 9:23).

18

The Faith Galaxy of Blood, Sweat, and Tears

And what shall I more say? for the time would fail me to tell of Gideon, and of Barak, and of Samson, and off Jephthae; of David also, and Samuel, and of the prophets:

Who through faith subdued kingdoms, wrought righteousness, obtained promises, stopped the mouths of lions,

Quenched the violence of fire, escaped the edge of the sword, out of weakness were made strong, waxed valiant in fight, turned to flight the armies of the aliens (Hebrews 11:32-34).

Faith takes on new dimensions in these verses. Yet they are part of the whole. You wouldn't understand faith if you didn't see these facets of it.

Take, for instance, this statement: *out of weakness were made strong* (v. 34). Men who had no courage, no strength, no ability—in their weaknesses faith caused them to be the opposite. No longer weak and defeated, they moved into a positive position through the power and strength of faith.

They were cowards, but God said, "No, you can do something else. You can fight, and you can win."

Then they *waxed valiant* [that's brave] *in fight, turned to flight the armies of the aliens.*

God said they did what they did by the power of faith. If God said it, we must accept it. It might cause us to see the whole world and all of history in a different way. We might have to come to realize that men such as General Montgomery and General Eisenhower actually won a war through faith.

Gideon

God said Gideon had faith. Judges 6:11 introduces this man:

> *And there came an angel of the LORD, and sat under an oak which was in Ophrah, that pertained unto Joash the Abiezrite: and his son Gideon threshed wheat by the winepress, to hide it from the Midianites.*

Gideon was hiding from his enemies. He wasn't courageous. But he became a warrior and the sixth judge of Israel. The Bible says he did it by faith.

Gideon's faith is seen when God finally convinced him to go out to war. But he was difficult to convince. First he had to have a fleece of wool all wet and the ground around it dry (Judges 6:37). Then he had to have the ground wet and the fleece dry. You might say he threatened God twice to see for sure if God wanted him to do it.

When he finally went out, thirty-two thousand men gathered to help. God looked them over and said,

"Gideon, this is too many." Now the enemy forces numbered one hundred thousand or more. But God said thirty-two thousand were too many—Israel might think they had won in their own strength (Judges 7:2). He told Gideon to send everybody home who was fearful and didn't want to fight. The ranks quickly reduced to ten thousand.

But God said, "You've still got too many."

Gideon said, "Lord, can't You count? I've only got ten thousand left."

"Too many!"

Then He tried them for Gideon. He said, "Send them to get a drink of water. Keep those who lap water with their tongues as a dog with their armor still in their hands. Send those home who lay down their armor and get down on their knees to drink."

Out of ten thousand, three hundred were left.

That's where some would lose heart. But that's where the power of faith came in. The strength of faith is not out there when you are winning the battle. The strength of faith is in the matter of decisions. Gideon's faith showed when he said, "I won't quit. Even though I had thirty-two thousand reduced to ten thousand, I won't quit." When that was reduced to three hundred, he said, "I still won't quit."

> *The strength of faith is not out there when you are winning the battle. The strength of faith is in the matter of decisions.*

Gideon took his three hundred—the strangest bunch of fighters you've ever seen. They all went home and got a pot out of their wives' kitchens. The pots were made of baked mud. Gideon told them to put a candle in each pot. Then he said, "When I blow the trumpet, hit the pot, and let your little light shine."

Now that didn't *seem* the way to win the battle. But it worked! When you think everything related to victory in your life has to be "two plus two equals four," you're wrong! God can make two plus two equal two hundred if He wants to. He can take that which is not and make it be. He can take that which does not exist and make it exist. God has power—sovereign power—to change things. No man can stop Him. This is when you know what faith really is. This is when you know whether or not a person has it. Those who do obey God.

Gideon's army broke their pots. The enemy saw the lights and began to fight each other. Gideon's men gave chase and received their enemy's wealth. There was a tremendous victory for God, and God called it faith.

Faith is courage. When you are reduced, you don't quit. Then when you are reduced again, you don't quit. When God says, "Go against a major enemy," you go. And you win. The victory is the fruit of faith.

Sometimes we only see the fruit of faith. We can't see what made it go. We say of men, "He's great. He has faith." But we have no idea what he went through behind the scenes. We only behold the fruit of his faith.

The fruit of faith tastes sweet. The bitterness was back there at decision-making time. If faith was not back there, there would never be any fruit to see.

> ## *The fruit of faith tastes sweet.*

We're so often blind to what *really* is faith and *really* makes faith work. All we see are the beautiful apples already grown, picked, polished, and on the shelf. Some would even rather have them cut up for them. They like it very comfortable.

But faith has to do with things that are sometimes terrible. God said Gideon won these battles by faith. God reduced him to such a small number. Man didn't do it—God did, because God wanted the glory for it. That's what faith is all about anyway: God getting the glory for something that should happen, and then it does happen.

Barak

God said Barak had faith. His faith is a little difficult to discover. Judges 4:6, 7 tells us about him:

> *And she* [Deborah] *sent and called Barak the son of Abinoam out of Kedesh-naphtali, and said unto him, Hath not the LORD God of Israel commanded, saying, Go and draw toward mount Tabor, and take with thee ten thousand men of the children of Naphtali and of the children of Zebulun?*
> *And I will draw unto thee. . . Sisera, the*

captain of Jabin's army, with his chariots and his multitude; and I will deliver him into thine hand.

Here a woman told a man what the Lord already had said. She put it in the form of a question: "Has not the Lord told you to do it?"

Deborah was a prophetess who judged the land of Israel. God's people were challenged to go to war. Their enemy had oppressed them twenty years with multitudes of people and nine hundred chariots of iron.

Deborah said, "Barak, has not God told you to go?"

Barak said, "I won't go unless you go."

Now I might accept as a form of weakness a man's saying he wouldn't go unless the lady went. What if men said, "Yes, I'll go fight for my country, but my wife has to come along, too"? There would be some unusual battlefields with thousands of men hanging on to their wives.

The remarkable thing is the Bible says Barak had faith. Where does his faith come in? It was inspired by a woman. She called him to what God had said—the Word of God—and he latched onto it.

They did go. Deborah went with him. The enemy's armies were defeated. Barak was not even permitted to destroy Sisera himself. Another woman was permitted to destroy him. Jael put a nail through his head (Judges 4:21).

Barak's faith was that if someone had heard from God, he would accept it. He had a meek spirit. He would be subject to someone else. And his faith was that when the Lord said, "Go," he went.

As I said, faith has so many avenues, so many dispositions, so many movements until it becomes a remarkable thing. It may be that each one of the four billion people on earth could have a different aspect of faith. That would mean faith is so inexhaustible all the preachers in the world would never get through telling about it.

Faith is so unique. It may be that your faith is separate from any other person who has lived, and my faith may be something God will never again duplicate. So let us allow faith to grow in our hearts, to increase until it becomes the motivating force that makes all our decisions. The Bible says it is what pleases God (Hebrews 11:6). We should develop our individual faith to bring the utmost pleasure to God.

> *Let us allow faith to grow in our hearts, to increase until it becomes the motivating force that makes all our decisions.*

Samson

In Samson's life we see some unusual movements of faith.

First, his mother, through communing with God, made him a Nazarite unto God from the day he was born. The three marks of Nazarites were: they did not touch the dead, they did not touch wine, and they did not cut their hair. Samson was to keep the vows of a Nazarite.

After he was grown, however, Samson lived a carnal life. He committed adultery with a harlot. He disclosed the secret of his strength to the pagan, Delilah. When his eyes were put out, he was in the wrong place with the wrong people.

But in-between all that, he did superhuman, supernatural feats. One time he tore a lion apart with his bare hands. Another time he carried away the gates of a city. Eight horses with a chariot could run through those gates. They were big and heavy. They were put into place by many animals pulling to get them into their sockets. No person who ever lived could pick up one of them, much less both of them. Yet Samson lifted them off their hinges and walked, not downhill, but uphill with them.

Samson did things that were phenomenal to the human race, things which have not been repeated.

We would say, "Oh, that's faith." No! That is the fruit of faith. Behind the fruit was a consecration to God. A man said, "I am consecrated to God. I am a Nazarite. I will not touch the dead. I will not drink wine. I will not cut my hair." Through this consecration Samson had strength no other human has paralleled.

God said Samson did what he did by faith. He trusted in God. He relied upon God.

Jephthah

Jephthah's story is very interesting. Judges 11:1 reveals how he was messed up before he got here: *Now Jephthah the Gileadite was a mighty man of valour, and he was the son of an harlot: and Gilead begat Jephthah.*

Jephthah's father was Gilead, for whom the entire area was named. But his mother was a harlot. His own family cast him out because of it. They said, "We don't want him here. He's a son born out of wedlock." So he went into another country to live.

But then the home folks got into war. They didn't have a brave man among them to lead them in battle, so they had to send for the one they had thrown out. He was a refugee. He lived with people of disrepute. But he came back with the disreputable ones and won a battle. He became a judge in Israel.

There is a remarkable attitude of faith in this man. He was willing to come back and help those who had cast him out and told him they never wanted to see him again.

Jephthah also trusted in God. He said, "Lord, even though I am nothing, I believe You can bring this victory." Jephthah brought a great victory for an entire nation. God said, "That is faith."

Samuel

It is easy to see why Hebrews 11:32 says Samuel had faith. He lived one of the most beautiful lives of anybody in the Bible. He was very spiritual. He was a priest, a prophet, and a government leader over the nation. He was outstanding in all aspects of leadership. He revealed tremendous faith throughout his life.

David

David, a man after God's own heart, is known as a man of faith, a king who trusted God.

Faith for Life Today and Resurrection Tomorrow

Hebrews 11:35 reveals two facets of faith at seemingly opposite sides of the spectrum: *Women received their dead raised to life again: and others were tortured, not accepting deliverance; that they might obtain a better resurrection.*

It is easy to see the faith of the widow during the ministry of Elijah, and of the Shunammite woman during the ministry of Elisha (1 Kings 17; 2 Kings 4). Hebrews says it was by their faith that they received their dead raised to life.

I know of two living examples of the rest of verse 35—one in Russia and one in Romania. Both are pastors under a government which says there is no God. Both have been imprisoned for their faith. Both have families who suffer with their fathers. The Russian's teenaged daughters live in constant danger. The Romanian's baby drinks sour milk when they can find it at all.

In both cases because of their widespread influence for Christ, the communist governments involved would like the pastors to leave the country. Deliverance has been offered. Each of the men—they don't know each other—has not accepted deliverance.

The Russian expressed it like this after having turned down deliverance for the third time: "God told me I could go if I want to. But His first will for my life right now is to stay here and head up this work." The Romanian expressed the same thing in different words. Both live lives of miracles and faith just to stay alive. But eternity will reveal a further more excellent fruit of their faith—a better resurrection!

Faith is trust. When you want to find faith, find trust. Trust is believing; and believing does the superhuman, the supernatural, that which the natural cannot do. The function of faith is to cause us to be what we normally would not be—and to cause us to perform what we normally could not perform.

> *Faith is trust . . . Trust is believing; and believing does the superhuman, the supernatural, that which the natural cannot do.*

God wants us to become people of faith so that when it comes to the great emergencies of life, we won't depend upon our brains. We won't depend upon the human. Our dependence will be upon the Lord.

God calls that faith, and He is pleased with faith. Let your trust be great. If you will, God will reward you for it. Those who have faith will be close to Him in heaven. It will be a great reception for Him to say, "Well done, thou good and faithful servant."

Part V

A Cloud of Witnesses Cheer Us on in Our Faith Exploits

19
Faith Has a Cloud of Witnesses

Wherefore seeing we also are compassed about with so great a cloud of witnesses, let us lay aside every weight, and the sin which doth so easily beset us, and let us run with patience the race that is set before us,

Looking unto Jesus the author and finisher of our faith. . . (Hebrews 12:1, 2).

It must make the devil angry that faith has a cloud of witnesses. He doesn't like faith. He tries to tell you it doesn't exist. He tries to say you don't have it when he knows you do. He doesn't want faith to have witnesses. But faith does possess "a great cloud of witnesses." That means there are a lot of them!

This chapter is different from the others. It is what I call an expository teaching of Hebrews 11:39 through 12:7:

And these all, having obtained a good report through faith, received not the promise:

God having provided some better thing for us, that they without us should not be made perfect.

Wherefore seeing we also are compassed about with so great a cloud of witnesses, let us lay aside every weight, and the sin which doth so easily beset us, and let us run with patience the race that is set before us,

Looking unto Jesus the author and finisher of our faith; who for the joy that was set before him endured the cross, despising the shame, and is set down at the right hand of the throne of God.

For consider him that endured such contradiction of sinners against himself, lest ye be wearied and faint in your minds.

Ye have not yet resisted unto blood, striving against sin.

And ye have forgotten the exhortation which speaketh unto you as unto children, My son, despise not thou the chastening of the Lord, nor faint when thou art rebuked of him:

For whom the Lord loveth he chasteneth, and scourgeth every son whom he receiveth.

If ye endure chastening, God dealeth with you as with sons; for what son is he whom the father chasteneth not?

And these all, having obtained a good report. . . (v. 39). "These all" includes everyone named or unnamed who is mentioned in Hebrews, chapter 11. They all obtained a good report.

This report was not with man. Man might have looked upon these heroes of faith in a different way. Martin Luther and John Wesley were not popular with their neighbors. Even Jesus was not popular with His neighbors. His own townspeople tried to kill Him. And it wasn't for anything bad. It was because He read the Book of Isaiah and said, "This has now come to pass" (Luke 4).

In spite of many of their contemporaries who did not like these people of faith, the Bible says they obtained a good report. That report was not in their respective city halls. It was in the books of heaven. Between the two, I'd rather have a good report card up there. I'd rather hear God say, "Well done," than the world. The world's "well done" won't get you to heaven.

. . . through faith. . . . To obtain something means to get it. You don't naturally have it—you go and get it. They obtained their good report with God. Now how did they get this report? They got the good report *through faith.* Through believing. Through trusting. Through relying. Through sticking in there. It was not obtained by physical strength. It was not obtained by a keen mind. The good report was obtained through faith.

> **The people of faith of the Bible got the good report through faith. Through believing. Through trusting. Through relying. Through sticking in there.**

. . . received not the promise. . . . What was the promise? The Messiah! Every one of them, beginning with Abel, looked for the Messiah. Abel heard his parents tell how God promised the Seed of a woman

who would bruise the serpent's head. He thought possibly he was the one to do it. But he suddenly found out with a crack in the brain that he was not. None of these lived to receive that Supreme Promise in their earth walk. Could you retain your faith without getting to the end result? You know what you want. You know what you're looking for. You know what you're believing for. But you never get to the end result. These never got to the ultimate result.

God having provided some better thing for us . . . . What do we have? We have Jesus. The Messiah has already come. We have the glorious Son of God in our hearts. He's changed our lives. He took away lying, stealing, and adultery. He gave us life—and that more abundantly. We have a better thing than they in the indwelling Holy Spirit and the baptism of the Holy Spirit. Some of them knew what Joel prophesied, *And it shall come to pass afterward* [in the last days], *that I will pour out my spirit upon all flesh. . .* (Joel 2:28). And they were hanging onto it. We don't hang—we have the promise.

. . . that they without us should not be made perfect. Abel needs us! Noah needs us! Abraham needs us! God showed Abraham on Mount Moriah. He said, "Take your son home. I'm going to give My Son." But you and I have the reality of it. So they are not perfect without us. We have to say, "You looked forward to it; we have it. We walk in the fulfillment of your expectation in the earth." The magnificent things taking place today which we enjoy, these people looked forward to with great anticipation.

You and I walked right into it and received it.

But even now, until the last little end piece in this jigsaw puzzle is in place, it is not completed. The Body will not be perfect until everybody—from the Genesis saints to the saints who come in through the Great Tribulation—is compacted together. The whole Body is not there yet. So it can't be perfect until we're all together. But your faith added to Noah's faith, added to Abraham's faith, added to Moses' faith, and so on, makes faith perfect. It will make you want to have faith when you see that yours is necessary for the fulfilling of all the divine purposes of God.

> *The Body will not be perfect until everybody—from the Genesis saints to the saints who come in through the Great Tribulation—is compacted together.*

Wherefore seeing we also are compassed about with so great a cloud of witnesses. . . . It is easier to believe today than ever before. We have the cloud of witnesses. We have so much evidence stacked up before us. We have the history of faith and the glorious things God has done through people who trusted Him. Not just one, or two, but a cloud of witnesses attest to it.

We're not struggling with something that hasn't been tried, something nobody knows anything about. We've got a great cloud of witnesses compassed about us. That means they are in a circle, all the way around us. If we look behind, they are there. If we look ahead, they are there. If we look to the east or the west, they are there. Anywhere we look, there are witnesses—people who trusted God and got results.

. . . let us lay aside every weight. . . . This divides the men from the boys. Remember that word *wherefore,* because that's your treasure word. *Wherefore seeing we also are compassed about with so great a cloud of witnesses, let us lay aside every weight. . . .* He's still talking about faith.

Who is it that doesn't demonstrate faith? Those who are weighted down.

Weighted down with what? With unbelief. With fear. With circumstances. With Aunt Mary's testimony that it doesn't work: "Uncle Jack prayed and still died." With the love of this world. With the cares of this life. With sorrows. With griefs.

But God says, "Lay aside *every* weight." If you are carrying any weights, you have them because you want them. "Oh," you say, "that isn't true." Identical things can happen to two different people, and one goes up while the other goes down. It is not what happens to you; it is how you react to what happens. Our insides make us what we are. One said, "I couldn't go through it." But somebody else went sailing through.

. . . and the sin. . . . Some weights may not necessarily be sin, so God goes a little deeper. Faith will not wade around in sin.

. . . which doth so easily beset us. . . . To live a life of God's strength and power, you will have to lay

aside the weights and sin that so easily get you off the track. They easily throw you to one side until you're not in the main line anymore. You cannot be with God's greatest if you hang on to sin. You can only be with God's greatest when you live a clean, holy, pure, undefiled life.

> ***To live a life of God's strength and power, you will have to lay aside the weights and sin that so easily get you off the track.***

God said this, but preachers who preach it become identified. "He's a hard preacher," people say. But preachers are not supposed to tell you how sweet you are. They are supposed to tell you what God means for you to do.

. . . and let us run with patience the race that is set before us. . . . Run! That doesn't mean slow down. If you don't keep moving, the devil will grow his devil weeds all around you. *Run.* That means move!

> ***If you don't keep moving, the devil will grow his devil weeds all around you.***

Faith is movement. Faith is an act. Faith is not an idea, a dream, or a mental assertion. Faith is going somewhere, reaching for something, doing something.

Put a circle around the word *patience* in your Bible. There are so many quitters. Thousands say, "I've got faith." Then a few days later, they say, "Well, I guess I didn't have it." No, they had something else. It wasn't faith.

Life is called a race. Until you get to the finish line, life is a race set before you. Only by faith can you run it well.

Looking unto Jesus. . . . If you don't look unto Jesus, your faith will fall flat. If you look at people, whether Lester Sumrall or anybody else, you will get hurt and lose out. You will get discouraged and say, "They didn't do right. They didn't do this. They didn't do that." Keep looking straight into the eyes of Jesus. Why?

. . . *the author and finisher of our faith.* . . . Keep looking into the eyes of Jesus, because He is the beginner and the finisher of your faith. That means no party is related to your faith but you and Jesus. He started it and He will finish it. He conceived it and He will culminate it. Everything your faith will ever have is in Jesus—nowhere else. If you put your faith in a man or in any situation on earth, you will be let down. Jesus is the author and the completer of your faith.

. . . *who for the joy that was set before him endured the cross.* . . . This is almost unbelievable. It means He looked straight across those three days—He looked through the cross and the grave to the joy that was set before Him. He could say, "Go ahead, hit My back. It will be healed on the third day and will never hurt again. Nail Me to the cross. I don't mind this. I've got that coming."

If you can't see life that way, your faith will wobble and weaken. Even while someone is hurting you here and now, faith says, "That doesn't mean a thing to me. Man, I've got it made, right over there." The whole Bible supports that.

What if Joseph had given up halfway and quit? His own family and the nation of Egypt would have starved to death. But he didn't let down. He didn't quit no matter how dark it got. They could put him in a hole. They could put him in jail. They could lie on him. He had a dream! He lived by a dream. He said, "I dreamed that I was to be great, and I've got to be great. I've got to get out of this jail. I've got to be great." The day came when he walked out and he didn't stop halfway. He went straight to the throne and took a seat as prime minister of the nation.

I think there are many whom God was going to elevate to tremendous situations in this life, but they just failed to run their race. They failed to look to Jesus, the Author and the Finisher of their faith, and they didn't see the joy of what was on the other side in relationship to what was happening then.

. . . *despising the shame.* . . . The shame meant nothing to Jesus. People spit on Him and mocked Him, but He just said, "Let Me love you. Let Me bless you."

Don't let people shame you. Don't let people look down on you. Just say, "Darling, you need a sweet prayer. I'll just give you one right now," Just be so big until you have to look down on them to see them. Just be so great until whatever they do is like a little kitten messing around.

The shame meant nothing to Him. Romans spitting—what did it mean? That little pipsqueak governor with the backbone of a jellyfish—what did that mean to Jesus? They'd be in hell in a few days, and Christ would be King of kings and Lord of lords forever and ever!

Faith moves straight through such obstacles. Faith goes right by the derisions of others.

. . . and is set down at the right hand of the throne of God. For consider him that endured such contradiction of sinners against himself. . . . Now God says to consider Jesus Who endured the contradiction of sinners. You've heard the contradiction of sinners. This is how it sounds: "Oh, it doesn't do any good to go to church. It doesn't do any good to read the Bible." What do they know about it? Nothing!

. . . lest ye be wearied and faint in your minds. When you see people getting weary and faint, you know what they're doing. They're listening to the contradiction of sinners. They are associating with the wrong people. They are not listening to faith. They are not reading the Word. They are not allowing the great cloud of witnesses God has prepared to surround them. And they are losing out. God gives them a rebuke in the next verse.

Ye have not yet resisted unto blood, striving against sin. He says, "You haven't laid down your life yet. You haven't been nailed to a cross. Don't be pitying yourself." Some people run away and cry when someone just looks at them the wrong way. That doesn't hurt you. Smile back.

And ye have forgotten the exhortation which speaketh unto you as unto children. . . . We are the children of God. We are different from the world.

My son, despise not thou the chastening of the Lord, nor faint when thou art rebuked of him. If a problem comes, whip it down. God doesn't want any of us fainting.

For whom the Lord loveth he chasteneth, and scourgeth every son whom he receiveth. God tries us out. He proves us. If you think it was easy for Noah to have faith, you should have been there. He didn't win a single convert in a hundred and twenty years. That's a long time to preach and not get anybody. Thank God, he saved his own household, but he didn't win anybody else. That's pretty dark. But Noah stayed true. He believed, and he endured.

If ye endure chastening, God dealeth with you as with sons; for what son is he whom the father chasteneth not?

Perhaps this is the best chapter of all. It gives you the dark side and the light side. It gives you the bright side and the side you won't enjoy so much.

But you are not short on witnesses to the wonders of walking in faith. God is saying to you, "Look at these people and see what they have done." You can say, "God can do it all over again." Everything He has done, He can do now. Only your unbelief will keep Him from doing it for you. Only your unbelief will keep Him from changing your world.

Trust God. Let Him guide you in the ways of faith until you see Jesus face-to-face.

Now that we have examined the attributes of faith, what it is, and how to pursue it, with a great cloud of witnesses watching, let's take a more in-depth look at "how" to take dominion in our lives.

Part VI

Now Take Your Dominion!

20
Eight Steps for Taking Charge of Your Life

In our modern world, we tend to identify with large groups and avoid personal contact. People want to be associated with big organizations in order to maintain a certain distance from other individuals. Even in modern warfare, soldiers may never see the enemy. Their long-range guns and missiles make personal contact unnecessary.

There was a time in military history when men fought battles as individuals and won glory for fighting alone. For example, with only the jawbone of an ass, Samson slew a thousand of the enemies of Israel. Young David's startling confrontation with the giant Goliath is another example of individual combat. David slew the heavily armed enemy of Israel with a single stone from his slingshot.

Spiritual conflict requires individual involvement. To win in this battle, you personally must exercise dominion. When you realize that personal victory must be attained through personal conflict, you are on your way to achieving dominion.

> *Spiritual conflict requires individual involvement. To win in this battle, you personally must exercise dominion.*

Where can dominion be taken? How should dominion be used? You can and should exercise your Christ-given dominion in the following eight areas of your life:

1. The World of Sin

Take dominion over sin. You do not have to be a slave to sin or yield to temptation. In Romans 6:14 Paul said, *For sin shall not have dominion over you: for ye are not under the law, but under grace.*

Stand on that promise. In the face of temptation, say out loud, "Sin shall not have dominion over me. I choose to dominate over this temptation. I have dominion over sin according to the Word of God."

David prayed, *Order my steps in thy word: and let not any iniquity have dominion over me* (Psalm 119:133).

Make God's Word a part of your very being. Walk according to His Word. Then your steps will be ordered by the Lord, and you will be invested with power and authority.

2. The World of Business and Finance

God wants His people to have the attitude of Adam toward this world. He made everything for Adam and gave him the position of dominion over His creation. God created the wealth of the world—the silver and gold are His (Haggai 2:8).

Abram followed God and became Abraham, the blessed. His servant described Abraham's blessings as follows:

> *And he said, I am Abraham's servant.*
> *And the LORD hath blessed my master greatly; and he is become great: and he hath given him flocks, and herds, and silver, and gold, and menservants, and maidservants, and camels, and asses* (Genesis 24:34, 35).

The Bible says, *Abram was very rich in cattle, in silver, and in gold* (Genesis 13:2). Abraham was a prosperous businessman who did not allow his wealth to dominate him.

Abraham refused to allow his riches to create strife in his family or become a source of greed in his life. When the land could not support the herds of both Abraham and his nephew, Lot, because *their substance was great* (Genesis 13:6), Abraham gave Lot first choice of grazing land. He said, *Let there be no strife* (Genesis 13:8). Abraham was not selfish.

Abraham knew that God was the source of his riches, and he paid tithes of everything he owned (Genesis 14:20-23).

The New Testament declares that we who live by faith in Jesus Christ are the children of Abraham Galatians 3:9, 13, 14, 29). Part of that blessing includes financial prosperity and dominion.

> *The New Testament declares that we who live by faith in Jesus Christ are the children of Abraham . . . Part of that blessing includes financial prosperity and dominion.*

The devil seeks to dominate man's relationship to the earth in the area of finances and earthly possessions. But God wants His sons to prosper and to have an abundance for the work of the Kingdom.

A person with dominion in this area of prosperity knows how to do his job well and how to handle money. His motives are right, and he treats his fellowman with generosity. If his motives are selfish, then he is outside the realm of dominion and is being dominated by greed.

God's people should dominate their personal finances and not be dominated *by* them. We are to exercise responsibility over the financial resources required to reach the world with the good news of the Kingdom.

> *God's people should dominate their personal finances and not be dominated by them.*

3. The World of Demons

Divine authority for the Christian extends to a

realm unseen by the natural man. Dominion over devils is one of the greatest areas in which a child of God can express power.

Every disciple must know that his warfare is not physical, natural, or carnal. Paul said in Ephesians 6:12, *For we wrestle not against flesh and blood, but against principalities, against powers, against the rulers of the darkness of this world, against spiritual wickedness in high places.*

Your battle is in the spiritual world against the rulers of darkness. An aggressive warfare is being waged on all fronts by unseen and formidable foes. The Church must exercise dominion over the powers of the spiritual world in order to reach the masses of this generation for Christ.

> ***The Church must exercise dominion over the powers of the spiritual world in order to reach the masses of this generation for Christ.***

Christ's disciples must do what Mark 16:17 says: *And these signs shall follow them that believe; In my name shall they cast out devils. . . .*

Who are these devils? They are fallen angels who fell from heaven when Lucifer exalted himself (Isaiah 14:12-17; Ezekiel 28:11-19). These fallen spirits are in complete obedience to their master, Satan. Their job is to dominate humans, to cause them to rebel against God, to corrupt their thoughts, to ruin their lives, and ultimately to cause them to miss heaven.

The heathen in foreign lands are more aware of this world of spirit beings than many Christians. This ignorance places the disciple in a losing position in the battle of the spirit world. You must know your enemy in order to defeat him.

The ultimate success or failure of the Christian disciple will not be in the visible world but in the invisible. America's military is moving away from conventional warfare on the earth and turning toward fighting in outer space. The Church, too, must move its battleground to the heavenlies against the prince and powers of the air.

The New Testament sets the divine pattern for dominion over devils. The apostles of the early Church set men and women free and wrought tremendous victories in the Kingdom of God. It must be the same today. Wherever and whenever a possessed person comes in contact with the Spirit-filled disciple, there must be a battle for deliverance.

The Lord Jesus Christ has given you authority— the right to command. He also has given you power— the right to act. May you never fail to use this delegated dominion to set men and women free by His power.

You can rejoice in the fact that the day is coming when the devil will be bound. The Apostle John said in Revelation 20:1-3:

> *And I saw an angel come down from heaven, having the key of the bottomless pit and a great chain in his hand.*

And he laid hold on the dragon, that old serpent, which is the Devil, and Satan, and bound him a thousand years,

And cast him into the bottomless pit, and shut him up, and set a seal upon him, that he should deceive the nations no more, till the thousand years should be fulfilled: and after that he must be loosed a little season.

What a glorious hour when there will be no devil, no sin, and no sickness. But until that hour, use your Christ-given dominion to paralyze Satan in every confrontation.

> ***Use your Christ-given dominion to paralyze Satan in every confrontation.***

4. The World of Thoughts

The human mind is the greatest arena of battle in spiritual conflict:

(For the weapons of our warfare are not carnal, but mighty through God to the pulling down of strong holds;)

Casting down imaginations, and every high thing that exalteth itself against the knowledge of God, and bringing into captivity every thought to the obedience of Christ (2 Corinthians 10:4, 5).

Dominion for the disciple includes bringing every thought into captivity and making it obedient to Christ. Every thought is to be controlled and lined up with the Word of God.

When Satan injects thoughts of doubt or fear, they are to be brought into captivity and cast out with the Word of God.

When he tempts you to fear, just stop and say, *God hath not given us the spirit of fear; but of power, and of love, and of a sound mind* (2 Timothy 1:7).

A fearful mind is not a sound mind. Rebuke fearful thoughts. A doubtful mind is not a sound mind. Cast out doubts with the Word of Christ.

Our minds are not to be garbage containers. If they are, our thoughts will be manifested in our words and actions. Do not entertain evil thoughts. The devil may inject an unclean idea or a negative thought into your mind, but you do not have to allow it to stay. Do not pet it and toy with it. Cast it out immediately and replace it with a thought that meets all these scriptural criteria:

> *Finally, brethren, whatsoever things are true, whatsoever things are honest, whatsoever things are just, whatsoever things are pure, whatsoever things are lovely, whatsoever things are of good report; if there be any virtue, and if there be any praise, think on these things* (Philippians 4:8).

If a thought is not true, honest, just, pure, lovely,

and of good report, simply refuse to allow it to stay in your mind.

This is an area where every disciple can and must assert dominion. You can bring into captivity every wild and unspiritual thought.

5. The World of Health and Healing

Sickness and disease can be made to obey the word of power and authority. In the Great Commission Jesus said, *These signs shall follow them that believe; In my name . . . they shall lay hands on the sick, and they shall recover* (Mark 16:17, 18).

Centuries before Christ, God declared that sickness is a curse (Deuteronomy 28). Many Christians do not realize this. Some people think sickness can be a blessing in certain cases. But God calls it a curse. It is a curse that follows the broken law.

If Jesus Christ had not died for us, we would certainly come under the curse of sickness with no hope of dominion over poor health. But God's great plan of redemption redeemed us from the curse of the law, including the curse of sickness: *Christ hath redeemed us from the curse of the law, being made a curse for us: for it is written, Cursed is everyone that hangeth on a tree* (Galatians 3:13).

> *God's great plan of redemption redeemed us from the curse of the law, including the curse of sickness.*

When Jesus was offered on Calvary's tree as the supreme sacrifice for man's sin, the veil of the temple sectioning off the holy of holies was rent in two from top to bottom. God will never again dwell in temples made with human hands.

Today every believer is actually the temple of God. Through the power of the Holy Spirit, God's glorious presence now inhabits a living temple (John 14:23; 1 Corinthians 3:16; 2 Corinthians 6:16).

God was particular about every detail of His dwelling place in the Old Testament. How much more must He be concerned about your body—the living temple for whom Christ died.

> *What? know ye not that your body is the temple of the Holy Ghost which is in you, which ye have of God, and ye are not your own?*
>
> *For ye are bought with a price: therefore glorify God in your body, and in your spirit, which are God's* (1 Corinthians 6:19, 20).

God is glorified when you take dominion over sickness and disease in your body.

Satan is the author of sickness. Adam knew no sickness until he gave Satan the authority to enter the world with all of his evil merchandise—sin, death, sickness, disease, fear, poverty, lies, and so forth.

In the area of disease, there is *authority* and *counterauthority.* The devil has power to bring disease upon you, as he did with Job. But as a Christian, you possess divine authorization to rebuke, renounce, and destroy all the power of the enemy.

You must exercise your rights, however. Sickness and disease do not automatically stay away from every believer.

Quote the source of your power. A policeman can say, "In the name of the law, stop!"

As Christ's disciple you must say, "In Jesus' name, I am healed!"

God promised that none of the diseases of Egypt would come upon His people. He revealed Himself as *Jehovah-Rapha—I am the LORD thy physician,* or *I am the LORD that healeth thee* (Exodus 15:26). The Old Testament is filled with the promises and provisions of God's healing power.

When Jesus came into the world, He destroyed the works of the devil—including sickness. *For this purpose the Son of God was manifested, that he might destroy the works of the devil* (1 John 3:8).

Jesus said, *Behold, I give unto you power . . . over all the power of the enemy: and nothing shall by any means hurt you* (Luke 10:19).

Christians who are not grounded in the Word are not aware of their dominion in such a strategic area. They do not know they have the authority to resist the devil and his works. *Resist the devil, and he will flee from you* (James 4:7).

The devil is an expert in guerilla warfare. He sneaks in unaware, coming in camouflage. He is a deceiver, using deception to create fears, phobias, confusion, and feelings of helplessness. Man receives these terrible things, not because the devil cannot be overcome but because man listens to the devil's voice.

6. The World of Sex

The Bible has a lot to say about the union between a man and a woman. God performed the first wedding ceremony uniting Adam and Eve. He told them to be fruitful and multiply and replenish the earth. In this way, God permitted man to join Him in divinity and in the mystery of life. Many mysteries surround mankind, but the greatest is how two protoplasmic cells unite and generate life.

Sex is the most intimate relationship between humans. And only the sexual relationship has the potential for creating an immortal soul. From the beginning, God has been very protective about sex. He addressed Himself to it very clearly in His Word. God's moral nature has never altered, and He does not change His moral standards to suit a self-indulgent generation.

Since the Garden of Eden, Satan has sought to degrade man in the area of sex. All forms of perversion, homosexuality, and moral uncleanness are contrary to God's laws of nature.

Men and women who do not exercise dominion in the area of sex cannot dominate in any area of life. Instead, they are dominated and become the victims of frustration, condemnation, regret, mental depression, and physical problems.

God wants people to be free from all abnormalities and immoral bondage. The person of dominion walks free in this area of sex.

7. The World of Family

God ordained the family. From the beginning, He intended mankind to exercise authority in the home. The Garden of Eden was Adam's home, and he was told to dress and guard it. Adam should not have allowed Satan to enter his home. He had the authority to keep the enemy out.

We have the authority to keep the devil out of our gardens. Take the name of Jesus and the sword of the Spirit and put Satan on the run every time you see his ugly head appearing. He has to flee.

> *Take the name of Jesus and the sword of the Spirit and put Satan on the run every time you see his ugly head appearing.*

If you have young children, or plan to have them, determine to train them up in the way they should go. God chose Abraham as the father of Israel because He knew he would teach his children the ways of righteousness (Genesis 18:18, 19). Many fine young parents today are bringing up their children from infancy on the milk of God's Word. They speak of the Lord in their homes at all times.

Perhaps your children are older. Maybe they were into trouble before you became knowledgeable in the things of God. God's Word says that children are a blessing from the Lord. Claim that promise. Take the name of Jesus, and break the power of the devil over your children. Then claim them for Jesus Christ, and begin to look at them in faith and love.

Your home is to be a haven of peace and love. Discipline yourself to walk in love there. Walk in the thirteenth chapter of First Corinthians, and you will walk in dominion in your family life.

> ***Walk in the thirteenth chapter of First Corinthians, and you will walk in dominion in your family life.***

Christian dominion by the blood of the Lord Jesus Christ is not only meant for this life but for the world to come. The Word of God teaches that we will carry dominion into the world beyond.

> *And the kingdom and dominion, and the greatness of the kingdom under the whole heaven, shall be given to the people of the saints of the most High, whose kingdom is an everlasting kingdom, and all dominions shall serve and obey him* (Daniel 7:27).

Kingdoms and dominion will be given to the victorious saints. We will be kings and priests forever!

> *And from Jesus Christ, who is the faithful witness, and the first begotten of the dead, and the prince of the kings of the earth. Unto him that loved us, and washed us from our sins in his own blood,*

And hath made us kings and priests unto God and his Father; to him be glory and dominion for ever and ever. Amen (Revelation 1:5, 6).

In the future life, the victorious disciple is to be a king and a priest. This dominion includes the material realm as well as the spiritual.

Take your place of authority in every area of your life, and victory will be yours both now and in eternity.

21
Eliminating Seven Deadly Fears

My mother, Betty Sumrall, was a person of dominion. Fear had no place in her life. I observed her life for fifty years. When the odds were great against her, she knew she would win. My mother was sure of the Word and convinced that God was performing His promises. She lived a victorious life of dominion.

Dominion is available to every believer. The decision is yours. Decide to be victorious in Jesus! Some people refuse to exercise the dominion God has given them through Christ Jesus. They are afraid to step out and take authority over the problem areas of their lives.

Acts 1:25 says that *by transgression* Judas failed. It was not an accident. There was no weakness on God's part or an insufficient supply of power. Judas fell because he refused dominion. He yielded himself to the devil, and in so doing he lost his life.

We all know people who have refused to exercise divine dominion. Some die premature deaths. Others fail in business or permit the devil to destroy their homes.

The devil would like to attack your dominion through *fear* in these seven areas:

211

1. Fear of change

A person who refuses change grows old quickly. We say he is "set in his ways," but this literally means he refuses to change. Fear of changing jobs, fear of moving to a new location, or fear of making new friends often destroys the power of dominion. Many people could be prosperous and victorious if they were not fearful of change.

2. Fear of people

It is the devil's trick to make us afraid of people. Nehemiah's enemies tried to make him afraid. Nehemiah responded to their hired prophet, *Should such a man as I flee* [or run and hide]? (Nehemiah 6:11). Nehemiah knew dominion and had no fear.

Sometimes people fear their boss because he is overbearing or demanding. Other people are afraid to witness to their neighbors about their relationship with Jesus.

God told His prophet Jeremiah, *Be not afraid of their faces: for I am with thee* (Jeremiah 1:8). We must never fear people.

> *Be not afraid of their faces: for I am with thee (Jeremiah 1:8). We must never fear people.*

3. Fear of the unknown

A person can never have dominion if he fears the

unknown. God commands the unknown, and His positive power is stronger than any negative force. Rest in the fact that God has His hand on tomorrow, and you need not be afraid of the unknown.

In Numbers, chapter 13, twelve select leaders of Israel were sent into Palestine to spy out the Land of Promise. Ten of them returned with what the Bible calls an "evil report."

They said, in effect, "The land is good, and the country is beautiful. It is rich and desirable, but giants live there." They told Moses, "We are like grasshoppers before them" (Numbers 13:32, 33).

The nation of Israel accepted the spies' evil report. They had forgotten how God brought them out of Egypt—not through their strength but in His power. They had forgotten the miracles that took place in the desert. Now they refused the dominion that belonged to them, and they turned back into the Sinai desert. For forty years they wandered around in a waterless land until they all died. Not one of the adults who accepted that report of fear entered the Promised Land.

God had said, "The land is yours."

The devil had said, "You are too small, too weak, and too insignificant."

The Israelites obeyed the wrong source of information, and their fear of the unknown kept them from receiving God's promises.

4. Fear of responsibilities

No one can enjoy dominion if he fears to take on

greater responsibilities. If you are willing to stay at the bottom because you cannot accept responsibility, you will never know the joys of dominion.

5. Fear of failure

Nothing destroys the power of dominion like the stalking fear of failure. The devil fosters fear, but the Spirit of Jesus does not know failure. When we are linked with Him, it is impossible to fail. Fear of failure comes from the devil and must be destroyed before you can enjoy the rewards of dominion.

> *When we are linked with God,*
> *it is impossible to fail.*

6. Fear of added work

You would be amazed at the millions of people who are fearful of what added work would do to them. They do not realize that while they are worrying about it, they could be accomplishing something worthwhile. Additional work brings spiritual and material growth. The devil's fears are always exaggerated and erroneous, so never be afraid of taking on added jobs.

7. Fear of physical or mental breakdown

Many men and women are tormented by the fear of having a breakdown. They fear the disintegration of their strength and moral courage. Job said that what he greatly feared came upon him (Job 3:25).

We must rebuke all such fear and be part of that select group who take their dominion. *For God hath not given us the spirit of fear; but of power, and of love, and of a sound mind* (2 Timothy 1:7).

Rebuke the devil, and he will flee from you. Rebuke fear, and it will flee from you. Once fear is deflected in your life, you can become the person of power God wants you to be.

22
You Are an Authorized Dealer of Dominion

People don't like substitutes. An automobile dealer displays a sign over his business that reads, "Authorized Dealer." The sign means a consumer can expect genuine parts for his car and factory-trained mechanics to install them—and no substitutes.

In the spiritual world, Bible-believing Christians are God's "authorized dealers" of His dominion. It would be most fitting for a church to display a sign saying, "Authorized Dealer of God's Spirit and Power."

> *In the spiritual world, Bible-believing Christians are God's "authorized dealers" of His dominion.*

Is the victorious life of Christian dominion only for the chosen few or is it for every disciple who receives Christ as Lord and Savior?

In his epistles to the churches, the Apostle Paul repeatedly spelled out the privileges and blessings belonging to each child of God.

Blessed be the God and Father of our Lord Jesus Christ, who hath blessed us with all spiritual blessings in heavenly places in Christ (Ephesians 1:3).

Dominion is for every believer who will accept the responsibility for exerting it.

Robbed of Rule

After a person is born again, the devil seeks in every way possible to hide the believer's position of authority from him. When the believer is aware of his privileges and power, Satan is completely defeated and his works are destroyed.

An age-long strategy of the devil is to attack the believer in the area of confession. He knows a person will never rise above his confession. Instead of making the promises of God his confession of faith, the believer constantly confesses his sickness, faults, and weaknesses. Since a man is what he confesses himself to be, the devil uses this means to keep the believer in bondage.

Satan does not want you to confess your position of dominion in Christ or your victories by the blood of God's Son. When you make these your confession, you exert dominion, authority, and power.

Three Hindrances to Dominion

These major hindrances can keep you from experiencing victory in your rightful realm of dominion.

First, ignorance is a real stumbling block to obtaining spiritual authority. A person cannot possess something he does not know he has. You could be willed an estate worth a million dollars, yet if you never learned about the will, you could die a pauper.

Second, unbelief can also keep you from entering this divinely appointed position of dominion. The children of Israel did not enter God's promised land of provision *because of unbelief* (Hebrews 3:19). God admonishes us to be careful lest we come short of entering His provision for the same reason (Hebrews 4).

Dominion is part of God's provision. But when a believer cannot trust the promises of God and does not stand spiritually and emotionally on what God has said, it is impossible to possess true dominion.

> *When a believer cannot trust the promises of God and does not stand spiritually and emotionally on what God has said, it is impossible to possess true dominion.*

Third, sin destroys man's position of dominion. When a person transgresses, he lowers himself from the limits and privileges God ordained for man in the Garden of Eden. Therefore, it is essential for a person to be cleansed by the blood of Jesus and to remain clean in order to exercise dominion.

The Spirit of Might

The Lord Jesus told His disciples that upon His

return to heaven, they would do the works that He did: *Verily, verily, I say unto you, He that believeth on me, the works that I do shall he do also; and greater works than these shall he do; because I go unto my Father* (John 14:12).

It is impossible to do the works of Jesus without the power of the Holy Spirit. Isaiah prophesied before the coming of the Lord Jesus that the Spirit of might would rest upon Him: *And the spirit of the LORD shall rest upon him, the spirit of wisdom and understanding, the spirit of counsel and might, the spirit of knowledge and of the fear of the LORD* (Isaiah 11:2)

Only Christ Himself is master of all dominion in heaven and earth. Consummating His colossal achievement of world redemption, the resurrected Christ proclaimed, *All power is given unto me in heaven and in earth* (Matthew 28:18).

What unlimited, unrivaled, and incalculable dominion and strength are involved in that universal proclamation.

Christ is unlimited! His power is omnipotent! His presence is omnipresent!

The believer's authority on the earth is staggering. Only Deity sets its limits, and heaven backs its God-given dominion. God wants to give every believer the Spirit of might so we can do the same works Jesus did.

The Apostle Paul prayed for the believers at Colosse that they might be *fruitful in every good work. . . . Strengthened with all might, according to his* [God's] *glorious power* (Colossians 1:10, 11).

Keys of the Kingdom

Only Christ Himself can set the boundaries or categories of dominion for His disciples. These boundaries are clearly defined by the Savior and recorded in the New Testament:

> *And I say also unto thee, That thou art Peter, and upon this rock I will build my church; and the gates of hell shall not prevail against it.*
>
> *And I will give unto thee the keys of the kingdom of heaven: and whatsoever thou shalt bind on earth shall be bound in heaven: and whatsoever thou shalt loose on earth shall be loosed in heaven* (Matthew 16:18, 19).

What are these keys of the Kingdom—which represent authority and dominion—given by the Lord Jesus Christ?

The early Church had power, and the known world was shaken by the power Christ promised His followers: *Ye shall receive power, after that the Holy Ghost is come upon you* (Acts 1:8).

Peter used the keys of the Kingdom when he preached the great prophetic message in Acts, chapter 2. The Church was birthed, and the first group of saints were filled with the Holy Spirit.

On that day Peter said, *For the promise is unto you, and to your children, and to all that are afar off, even as many as the Lord our God shall call* (Acts 2:39).

These words clearly reveal that this dominion was not only for the apostles. It was for the thousands of people who heard Peter's sermon on the day of Pentecost. It was for their children, and it was for those afar off—even us today.

Peter used a key of dominion at the Gate Beautiful of the temple in Jerusalem. A man lame from birth was brought daily to the gate to beg alms. Then one day things changed for him. As he looked intently upon Peter and John, he heard Peter speak these words of dominion: *In the name of Jesus Christ of Nazareth rise up and walk* (Acts 3:6).

Strength and dominion were the norm in the early Church.

These keys of the Kingdom are still available to the Church of Jesus Christ. The ministry of binding and loosing belongs to the Church. Whatever is bound on earth will be bound in heaven. Whatever is loosed on earth will be loosed in heaven.

Repeatedly, the New Testament emphasizes that this divine dominion was not given exclusively to the apostles.

Stephen, a deacon in the church of Jerusalem, possessed such great dominion that he *did great wonders and miracles among the people* (Acts 6:8).

Philip was also a deacon in the church of Jerusalem, and people were healed and set free through his ministry.

Then Philip went down to the city of Samaria, and preached Christ unto them.

And the people with one accord gave heed unto those things which Philip spake, hearing and seeing the miracles which he did.

For unclean spirits, crying with loud voice, came out of many that were possessed with them: and many taken with palsies, and that were lame, were healed.

And there was great joy in that city (Acts 8:5-8).

I have always encouraged the lay members of the churches I have pastored to pray for themselves and for others, expecting answers from God. Many miracles of healing and deliverance have resulted through the prayers of simple, Spirit-filled people.

Clearly, dominion is not for a select few. It is for every disciple of the Lord Jesus Christ.

23
Using Your Weapons of Victory

A soldier is never sent into battle until he has a complete understanding of the weapons of his warfare. Unless a soldier knows the power of his weapons and the range of their effectiveness, he is not capable of routing the enemy and experiencing victory.

Until a Christian disciple understands the weapons of his dominion, he cannot effectively use them. The Christian must know what to do and when to do it in order to win the necessary victory.

Jesus Christ has given to His disciples all the weapons necessary for dominion on this earth. The arena of conflict, however, is in the spiritual realm.

> *Jesus Christ has given to His disciples all the weapons necessary for dominion on this earth.*

For we wrestle not against flesh and blood, but against principalities, against powers, against the rulers of the darkness of this world, against spiritual wickedness in high places (Ephesians 6:12).

Weymouth's Translation says our conflict is with *the despotisms, the empires, the forces that control and govern this dark world—the spiritual hosts of evil arrayed against us in the heavenly warfare.*

Our battle is not with "flesh and blood." Our battle is not with humans or denominations or organizations. Our battle is spiritual.

The conflict is spiritual and so are the weapons: *For though we walk in the flesh, we do not war after the flesh: (For the weapons of our warfare are not carnal, but mighty through God to the pulling down of strong holds)* (2 Corinthians 10:3, 4).

Learn to use the following God-given weapons of spiritual warfare:

1. The Word of God

Every victorious Christian must learn how to use the Bible effectively. The Word of God is alive, powerful, and sharp (Hebrews 4:12). The Bible is your "sword" (Ephesians 6:17). With God's Word in your heart and in your mouth, you will dominate Satan.

> **With God's Word in your heart and in your mouth, you will dominate Satan.**

Revelation 1:16 pictures Jesus with a sharp two-edged sword coming out of His mouth. He used this weapon to defeat Satan in the wilderness. Jesus

226

declared, *It is written. . . . It is written again. . . .* And the third time, *Get thee hence, Satan: for it is written. . .* (Matthew 4:4, 7, 10). Like Jesus, we can use this sword with our mouths against the enemy (Revelation 19:15).

The Bible is infallible and inspirational. It is inerrant in its information and supernatural in its application to daily living. But God's Word must be read and studied before it can be effective in our lives.

When I was in France on a preaching tour, a very lovely French lady came up to me and said, "I want you to know that I'm safe."

I must have looked confused because she went on to explain, "I bought a Bible yesterday and put it in my mailbox."

"In your mailbox?" I repeated.

She said, "The devil will have to pass by the mailbox to get to me. With the Bible inside it, he can't hurt me anymore."

I said, "You better sit down and let me tell you a little more about the Bible. We don't believe in using God's Word like a lucky charm. The Word of God must be read and studied in order to be effective in your life. You must get it into your heart. God's Word only works on the inside of the believer, not in the mailbox."

In my personal life the Bible has been a true guide in every crisis. When God wants to lead me in a new direction, He directs me through His Word. The Bible is my source book for truth. When I want to know what is right and wrong, I refer to what the Bible says about the matter.

You can be a mighty man or woman of God by giving the Word first place in your life. If you feed your spirit daily on the Word of God, you will grow spiritually (1 Peter 2:2). Your spirit, strong and well-nourished, will dominate your being. Rather than being ruled by the outward man, the inner man will rule over your mind, will, emotions, and flesh. You will know your God and do exploits in His name.

> ***You can be a mighty man or woman of God by giving the Word first place in your life.***

2. The Name of Jesus

Jesus gave the Church His name. The name of Jesus is above every name. At that name, beings in heaven, in earth, and under the earth must bow (Philippians 2:9-11). That name is dominion!

Before He was crucified, Jesus spoke to His followers of the soon-coming day when He would give them the power of attorney to use His exalted name. They would use it in prayer (John 16:23, 24).

Jesus spoke of His followers doing the works that He did, and greater works, because He was going unto His Father. In the next breath He said, *Whatsoever ye shall ask in my name, that will I do, that the Father may be glorified in the Son. If ye shall ask any thing in my name, I will do it* (John 14:13, 14).

After His death, burial, and resurrection, and before He ascended to sit down at the right hand of the Father, Jesus told His disciples to *Go . . . and teach all nations* (Matthew 28:19).

The Gospel of Mark records the signs that would follow the believers as they carried out Jesus' orders:

> *In my name shall they cast out devils; they shall speak with new tongues;*
> *They shall take up serpents; and if they drink any deadly thing, it shall not hurt them; they shall lay hands on the sick, and they shall recover* (Mark 16:17, 18).

That's dominion! And it's all in His name! Every soldier of the cross who walks in victory and dominion knows that he possesses this mighty weapon and he knows how to use it.

3. Faith

Without dynamic faith born in the heart at conversion and nourished through the Word of God, a believer cannot successfully engage in battle with demon power and win.

When Jesus came down from the mount where He was gloriously transfigured, He was met with the news that His disciples had been unable to cast the devil out of a certain man's lunatic son. His first reaction to the report was, *O faithless and perverse generation* (Matthew 17:17).

The devil departed, of course, at Jesus' command.

His disciples asked Jesus, *Why could not we cast him out?* (v. 19).

Jesus responded, *Because of your unbelief . . . If ye have faith as a grain of mustard seed, ye shall say unto this mountain, Remove hence to yonder place; and it shall remove; and nothing shall be impossible unto you* (v. 20).

When a person is challenged by temptation, disease, or the devil, his faith must constantly come into focus. He must have faith to command God's power.

When God told Abraham He was going to destroy Sodom and Gomorrah, Abraham reasoned with God. He stood before the Lord and said,

> *Wilt thou also destroy the righteous with the wicked?*
> *Peradventure there be fifty righteous within the city: wilt thou also destroy and not spare the place for the fifty righteous that are therein?*
> *That be far from thee to do after this manner, to slay the righteous with the wicked. . . . Shall not the Judge of all the earth do right?* (Genesis 18:23-25).

God agreed to Abraham's request and said He would not destroy those wicked cities for the sake of fifty righteous people. Abraham decreased the number of the righteous to forty-five, then forty, then thirty, then twenty, and finally to ten. Each time the Lord was willing to meet Abraham's conditions.

The true power of faith never has been fully utilized by man. God is still waiting for heroes of faith to use the divine dominion He gave to Adam in the Garden of Eden.

> ***The true power of faith never has been fully utilized by man.***

In the New Testament Church, it was the force of faith that caused Peter to turn to the body of a dead woman and say, *Tabitha, arise* (Acts 9:40). It was by faith that the Apostle Paul commanded the spirit of divination to come out of the fortune-telling damsel (Acts 16:18).

Faith is the key that unlocks the generosity and strength of God. Faith pleases God but *without faith it is impossible to please him. . .* (Hebrews 11:6).

Faith has been called the eye that sees the invisible, the ear that hears the inaudible, the hand that feels the intangible, and the power that works the impossible.

> ***Faith has been called the eye that sees the invisible, the ear that hears the inaudible, the hand that feels the intangible, and the power that works the impossible.***

Jesus said, *All things are possible to him that believeth* (Mark 9:23).

Faith works by the spoken word. Saying and believing go together, as Jesus explained:

Whosoever shall say unto this mountain, Be thou removed, and be thou cast into the sea; and shall not doubt in his heart, but shall believe that those things which he saith shall come to pass; he shall have whatsoever he saith (Mark 11:23).

Faith is an act. Martin Luther gave this view of faith: "It is a busy, active, living reality that does not ask, 'What shall I do?' but before it has time to ask, it is up and doing."

David believed Goliath would be defeated, so he hurled a stone at his head. *Faith acts.*

Faith is a way of life—a walk with God. The great miracles that characterized Smith Wigglesworth's ministry were the result of his close walk with God. He talked with God so often and for so long that when Smith made a request it was easy for God to understand. The tendency of many is to walk so far from God that it is not possible to hear Him when He speaks. But the person of dominion will walk with God and live out his faith. Living faith, the life of God, will flow from his innermost being.

How do you get faith? The rule is simply this: *Faith cometh by hearing, and hearing by the word of God* (Romans 10:17).

The Word alone is the source of faith. But the Word will not build faith unless it becomes a part of your very being. Jesus said, *If ye abide in me, and my words abide in you, ye shall ask what ye will, and it shall be done unto you* (John 15:7).

> **The Word alone is the source of faith. But the Word will not build faith unless it becomes a part of your very being.**

4. Prayer

Throughout history every outstanding man and woman of God has been a person of prayer. Prayer is one of the Christian disciple's most powerful weapons. In prayer, the believer receives the infilling of divine energy. After Jesus had prayed and fasted for forty days, He victoriously defeated Satan single-handedly in the greatest spiritual struggle ever recorded.

The prayer closet is actually the *council chamber* where divine commands are issued. In order to possess great dominion, you must constantly return to the Master to receive instructions from Him.

> **In order to possess great dominion, you must constantly return to the Master to receive instructions from Him.**

The prayer closet is the *heart-study place.* This is not where the mind learns, it's where the heart becomes instructive. In prayer we learn about God, His blessings, and His anointings.

Jesus told Peter, *Flesh and blood hath not revealed it unto thee, but my Father which is in heaven* (Matthew 16:17). We learn more in an hour of devotion and prayer than in many hours of searching libraries and seeking out man's wisdom. Divine revelation is brought into focus in the prayer closet. You won't find it anywhere else. Prayer is the key that unlocks the treasures of God.

Prayer is power.

Elijah demonstrated the dominion of prayer when he called upon God to send rain upon the land. The New Testament points out that Elijah was a man like we are. The difference is, he knew how to pray.

The early Church prayed, and the place where they were assembled together was shaken (Acts 4:31).

Paul and Silas prayed and sang songs in the inner cell of a Philippian jail at midnight. The strength of their prayer shook the jail itself and resulted in the salvation of the jailer (Acts 16:25-34).

The act of praying generates omnipotence. Prayer gives the frail human reed unshakable strength.

If you do not know how to pray, you do not know the power of God. Prayer is the most talked about, discussed, and the least used power available to mankind.

Oil, undiscovered, is an untapped resource. Coal, not mined, is an untapped source of power. But the greatest source of untapped power and resource is prayer. All that prayer can do has never yet been defined. This tremendous source of power has never been fully researched or developed.

> ## The greatest source of untapped power and resource is prayer.

In his article, "Man the Unknown," published in *Reader's Digest,* Dr. Alexis Carrel said: "As a physician, I have seen men, after all other therapy had failed, lifted out of disease and melancholy by the serene effort of prayer. It is the only power in the world that seems to overcome the so-called 'laws of nature.'"

Through personal communication with the Creator, you can do things you could never do before. Pray without ceasing, and you will know dominion in your life. Continual communion with the Commander assures victory.

5. Action

Dominion means *to do.* Dominion is an *act* and not an idea. God does not give power to the inactive. Jesus said, *He that believeth on me, the works that I do shall he do also* (John 14:12).

Throughout history, those who possessed dominion were men and women of action. God told Moses to stretch forth his rod, and the waters of the Red Sea rolled back, making a path for the children of Israel (Exodus 14).

Jesus told a man with a withered hand, *Stretch forth*

thine hand (Matthew 12:13). Jesus did the rest. The man's hand was restored whole like his other hand.

In most instances in God's Word, action was necessary before dominion was realized. The children of Israel had to march around Jericho before the walls collapsed. Naaman had to dip seven times in Jordan before his leprosy was cleansed.

Works alone are not sufficient for salvation or dominion. But some action is necessary—even vital.

> ***Works alone are not sufficient for salvation or dominion. But some action is necessary—even vital.***

Paul reminded the Corinthian Christians that there is work to do for the Kingdom of God: *For we are labourers together with God* (1 Corinthians 3:9).

In the second chapter of James, even stronger language is employed: *What doth it profit, my brethren, though a man say he hath faith, and have not works? Can faith save him . . . Even so faith, if it hath not works, is dead, being alone* (vv. 14, 17).

The word translated "works" here implies action. One translation reads, *Faith without corresponding actions is dead.*

It is not enough to know God's will—you must do it. *Not with eyeservice, as menpleasers; but as the servants of Christ, doing the will of God from the heart* (Ephesians 6:6).

Having money is not enough. Knowing you have it is not enough. You could know you had money in the bank and still go hungry and cold. You must go to the bank, withdraw some cash from your account, and spend it for food and warm clothing.

So it is with Christian dominion. Before it pays off with bountiful blessings, dominion must be put in force with action on the part of the believer.

Dominion is an instrument to better enable the disciple to work for God and to obey His commandments.

God's commandments have always been: *Go. Do. Give. Work.*

By using the pertinent weapons of dominion, any believer can be a triumphant Christian. Therefore, I urge you to stand up, use the instrument God has given you, and have dominion with Christ. Be an overcomer and a blesser of mankind all the days of your life.

24
Taking Your Rightful Position

God's Word says, *My people are destroyed for lack of knowledge. . .* (Hosea 4:6). Without knowledge of your true relationship with God, you cannot possess dominion over the many conflicts of life.

Suppose someone kidnaps a king's only son, the crown prince of the realm. Later, the child is abandoned. A beggar finds and adopts the boy, having no idea of his identity. Now the child of the king eats beggar's refuse, clothes himself in filthy rags, and begs from house to house.

But suppose the king knows the young prince by a birthmark that establishes his identity beyond question. The royal father never gives up his search for the prince.

One day the king hears that a child resembling his son lives in a distant city with a beggar. Arriving at the beggar's hovel, the king examines the child and finds him to be his son. The crown prince is washed and groomed. He is given a robe, a ring, and a place of authority in the kingdom.

Although he was the son of the king, the crown prince had lived for years like a beggar because he did not know who he was. He did not know his position of dominion.

Many Christians today are like this prince. They belong to Christ and are sons of God, yet the devil keeps them in ignorance so they will not realize their divine right of dominion. Once they understand the basis of their dominion in Christ, they live an empowered life of continual victories.

It is imperative that you know—and *know* that you know—your rights as a follower of the Lord Jesus Christ. You are entitled to dominion.

These steps gleaned from God's Word will help you take dominion in your personal life.

Recognize Your Source of Power

In Ephesians 1:17-23, Paul prayed a prayer for Christians. He specifically requested that God grant them *the spirit of wisdom and revelation* concerning certain vital truths. He knew they needed to understand some things. One thing he wanted them to know was: *What is the exceeding greatness of his power* to *us-ward who believe* (Ephesians 1:19).

You and I must understand the exceeding greatness of His power directed toward us who believe. We must know the exceeding greatness of God's power flowing through us.

Paul's prayer given by the Holy Spirit describes this mighty strength directed toward us as:

According to the working of his mighty power,
Which he wrought in Christ, when he raised
him from the dead, and set him at his
own right hand in the heavenly places,

Far above all principality, and power, and might, and dominion, and every name that is named, not only in this world, but also in that which is to come:

And hath put all things under his feet, and gave him to be the head over all things to the church,

Which is his body, the fulness of him that filleth all in all (Ephesians 1:19-23).

Recognize your source of power!

Your power comes directly from headquarters and headquarters is in heaven.

We have a daily source of strength and power the world knows nothing about. The world cannot tap it. The only way to get into this power is to get into Jesus. The only way to get into Jesus is to believe in Him. The only way to believe in Him is to accept Him as your Lord and Savior (Romans 10:9, 10). When Jesus becomes Lord of your life, this exceedingly great power is yours.

> ***Believers have a daily source of strength and power the world knows nothing about.***

Recognize your source. And recognize what is not your source. Your source is not the human mind. Your source is not human strength. Your source is God!

Recognize Your Need for the Church

The most powerful living organism on the earth

today is the Church—the very Body of Christ. Jesus Christ is the Head of this Body: *And he is the head of the body, the church: who is the beginning, the firstborn from the dead; that in all things he might have the preeminence* (Colossians 1:18).

Now ye are the body of Christ, and members in particular (1 Corinthians 12:27).

Jesus Himself described the irresistible strength of the Body: *I will build my church; and the gates of hell shall not prevail against it* (Matthew 16:18).

For many centuries the Church did not fully recognize her indomitable power. But you and I are living in a day when this powerful organism is waking up ready to arise and shine as the Prophet Isaiah foretold (Isaiah 60).

We are the Body of Christ, and we must accept our spiritual authority. We must realize that the gates of hell cannot prevail against the Church. As we move together, nothing can stand before us. We can change anything we want to change on the face of this earth.

Recognize your relationship to the Church, and be closely related to Christ's Body of believers. You cannot neglect the Body of Christ and be strong in the Lord. Your relationship with other believers is very important.

Some people say, "It doesn't matter if I go to church or not." That is a lie from the devil.

Believers minister to each other. People sitting in the pews have encouraged me as I preached. Something in me rose up as I looked at them. If they stayed home, I wouldn't have gotten that inspiration or received that blessing. At times I've been so blessed shaking someone's hand at church that I didn't want to let go.

People who stay home are selfish. You can never grow in God and be selfish.

> *Even when we were dead in sins,* [God] *hath quickened us together with Christ, (by grace ye are saved;) And hath raised us up together, and made us sit together in heavenly places in Christ Jesus* (Ephesians 2:5, 6).

We are to sit together in spiritual places in Christ Jesus.

A good friend of mine, who held a responsible position with a large firm, was asked to transfer to another area of the country. He was offered a much higher salary.

This man traveled to the area and searched for a church he liked. When he could not find one, he returned and said to his boss, "I don't want the new position."

His superior said, "Why don't you want the job? Isn't it good?"

He said, "I suppose it is. But I can't find a church I want to worship in at the new location. So I don't want the job."

His boss could not understand. This man refused the advancement because he couldn't find a church where he and his family could worship, learn, grow, fellowship, and work.

Thousands of Christians have backslidden because

they moved to places where they couldn't find a church that met their spiritual needs. Almost every day I hear someone say, "I can't find a good church where I live."

I say, "Why did you move there?"

The most important thing in life is your spirit, soul, and body—not your pocketbook. The most important thing for your children is to have a good church where they are taught God's Word.

Recognize your relationship with the living Body of Christ. That is the path of victory and dominion.

Identify Your Enemy

If you don't know who your enemy is, you won't be able to win a victory. You won't know where to deliver a blow.

> *If you don't know who your enemy is, you won't be able to win a victory.*

If you think your enemy is your wife, your husband, your children, or the church, you will never be able to win a victory. Striking out at the wrong foe only makes matters worse.

Moffatt's Translation describes our enemies as *the angelic rulers, the angelic authorities, the potentates of the dark present, the spirit-forces of evil in the heavenly sphere* (Ephesians 6:12).

First, identify your enemy. Satan is the enemy of God and the enemy of God's creation, mankind. When

Satan strikes at the human personality, it is imperative to recognize the source of the trouble.

Instead of getting grouchy and grumpy, get into a state of prayer and say, "Let me see here. My wife is a sweet person, so it is not her. This is from the devil. I am going to resist him."

Close your fist and say, "Satan, in the name of Jesus Christ of Nazareth, I command you to take your hands off my marriage. Get out of my house. And get out of here *now!*"

By saying this, you will have identified your enemy. You will have successfully stopped his tactics, and you won't be fighting against your family.

Know Your Enemy's Weakness

The devil is completely defeated by the Lord Jesus Christ. He can't do anything against Jesus. No devil or demon anywhere can combat the Holy Spirit. The early apostles brought great fear to demons who cried and ran away from the disciples' presence.

Any true believer can rebuke the devil today. He still has to flee when Christians resist him. *Submit yourselves therefore to God. Resist the devil, and he will flee from you* (James 4:7).

We do not necessarily have to fight the devil. We can simply remind him of Calvary where the Lord Jesus Christ defeated him. Remind him of his complete defeat and of his ultimate destiny—hell. Tell the devil, "Don't you know what is ahead of you? Don't you know where you are going to endure eternity?" Then tell him that you know he is a defeated foe.

Satan is limited. He is limited by his fallen state (At one time he was an archangel). Christ's resurrection cut him short and stripped from him the keys of hell and of death (Revelation 1:18).

Satan has a bruised head that cannot be healed. In the Garden of Eden, God foretold that the Seed of the woman was coming (Genesis 3:15). This Child of a virgin would bruise Satan's head and break Satan's lordship. The devil and all his cohorts know that Jesus Christ fulfilled this prophecy and brought them *to nought* (1 Corinthians 2:6-8).

All evil spirits, who were brought to nothing by the Lord of Glory, fear and tremble before any believer with the power, the anointing, and the authority of Jesus Christ.

> *All evil spirits, who were brought to nothing by the Lord of Glory, fear and tremble before any believer with the power, the anointing, and the authority of Jesus Christ.*

Do not talk about how big and strong the devil is. If you do, you will believe it. Instead, remind him that he has already lost the war. Remind him he is under your feet and you are walking on top of him (Ephesians 1:19-23). He understands that.

Stay Ready for Battle

We have an enemy whose key strategy is to keep the Christian away from his place of authority and spiritual power. Satan tries to keep us "off base."

Be aware of his tactics. Immediately resist and refuse to accept any of the following states Satan may try to put upon you.

Vexation. If Satan can keep you in an agitated state, you cannot cast out devils. If he can keep you angry with someone, you cannot heal the sick.

Learn to recognize the enemy's working in your life. Keep your mind on Jesus, and you will have perfect peace.

Depression. If the devil can get you depressed, you are not effective in the Kingdom. You cannot minister to others when your heart is weighed down.

Depression can come from many sources—from your home, at work, or in your body. Events can take place that make life seem hopeless.

You can get depressed listening to the news. If that happens, turn off the news and read two or three chapters in the Bible. News reports don't give a clear picture of things anyway. Most reporters give their ideas about things, and their ideas sometimes come from perverted minds.

Confusion. If the devil can get you confused, you will not be effective in God's Kingdom. Life is simple. You only have to make one decision at a time. If you ask God for wisdom, He will help you make each decision without confusion. But once you make a decision don't keep making it all day long. Don't take the dress back to the store forty times. Keep it when you buy it.

Stop for a moment and say, "My name is Sam Jones. My address is so-and-so. I work at such and such a place. I am married to Mary Jones, and I have so many children. I am saved and filled with the Holy Spirit. I belong to such and such church. Devil, I don't need to know much else, so get out of my way."

The devil does not want you to be ready for battle. He wants you in a state of confusion. If you are, you are not prepared to resist him.

You don't have to live in a state of confusion! The devil is a liar, and there is victory in Jesus!

Anything that is not clear today will be clear tomorrow. Rejoice in today, and God will bring peace and clarity out of confusion.

Selfishness. If the devil can get you to be self-centered and keep you looking at yourself, you will not be ready to be used by God. You will be constantly wondering, "How am I getting along? What can I do for myself? Me. . . . My. . . . Me. . . . My. . . ."

Be Christ-centered. Say, "Lord, I am out to win souls, and I don't mean maybe! Devil, we're coming after them. They belong to Jesus, and you can't have them!"

The devil would like Christians to be so self-centered about their business and homes that they lose the vision for saving the world.

The devil would like Christians to be so self-centered about their business and homes that they lose the vision for saving the world.

Many years ago when I was in China, a Chinese communist told me, "You have more missionaries than we have communists in China—but we are going to take China. Do you know why?"

I asked, "Why?"

He said, "You teach people to give 10 percent. We teach them to give 100 percent. I give everything to the party. We are going to win."

I just stared at him not knowing what to say. But I can assure you that as long as you are self-centered you are ineffective. Get lost in the great love of God, and lose your self-centeredness. Love the people of the world. Love the people of your community. Then you are ready to defeat the devil.

Recognize the Power of Praise

Jesus said,

> *Whatsoever ye shall bind on earth shall be bound in heaven: and whatsoever ye shall loose on earth shall be loosed in heaven . . . .*
> *For where two or three are gathered together in my name, there am I in the midst of them* (Matthew 18:18, 20).

The devil is subject to the believer's *faith,* and he cannot overcome it.

The devil is subject to the believer's *authority,* and

he must submit to it.

The devil is subject to the believer's *rights,* and he can't take them away.

The devil is subject to the *words* a believer speaks, and he must obey. If the believer tells the devil to go, he must go!

One of the most dramatic and powerful demonstrations of dominion is *singing.*

The entire nation of Israel sang a song of triumph as they crossed the Red Sea. *The Lord is my strength and song. . .* (Exodus 15:2).

Deborah and Barak sang a great song of victory (Judges 5).

Paul and Silas sang in the Philippian jail. Their shackles fell off and the gates flung open (Acts 16:25, 26).

Almost all nations have anthems that arouse national pride in their people. Armies sing military songs as they march into war.

New Testament believers are told: *Be filled with the Spirit; speaking to yourselves in psalms and hymns and spiritual songs, singing and making melody in your heart to the Lord* (Ephesians 5:18, 19).

God wants us to be glad and sing songs of victory. Go throughout life singing, "Jesus already has won! The Church already is victorious!"

If the devil says something about it, stop him by saying, "Shut up, in Jesus' name. We have already won the battle!"

There is victory in Jesus. Whatever you need, He has already won for you. Just claim what is yours in His name.

> ***There is victory in Jesus. Whatever you need, He has already won for you. Just claim what is yours in His name.***

If you are sick, say, "I thank You, Father, that Jesus has obtained my healing. I receive it now in His name. Thank You. I have it now."

Remember! *You are what God says you are! You can do what God says you can do!*

25
Supreme Authority

No other person ever asserted dominion like the Lord Jesus Christ. He knew divine dominion. *For in him dwelleth all the fulness of the Godhead bodily* (Colossians 2:9).

Our Lord Jesus had dominion in every stage of His life.

His virgin birth, first spoken of in the Garden of Eden, had been prophesied through the Prophet Isaiah 750 years before the Babe lay in the manger: *Therefore the Lord himself shall give you a sign; Behold, a virgin shall conceive, and bear a son, and shall call his name Immanuel* (Isaiah 7:14).

His supernatural birth transgressed the laws of nature:

> *And the angel answered and said unto her, The Holy Ghost shall come upon thee, and the power of the Highest shall overshadow thee: therefore also that holy thing which shall be born of thee shall be called the Son of God* (Luke 1:35).

The One Who had lived through all eternity—the One Who was with God and was God—the One by whom all things were made—became flesh and dwelt among us (John 1:1-4, 14).

Through the power of the Holy Spirit, Jesus entered an earthly body so He could defeat Satan for us.

> *Wherefore when he cometh into the world, he saith, Sacrifice and offering thou wouldest not, but a body hast thou prepared me:*
>
> *In burnt offerings and sacrifices for sin thou hast had no pleasure.*
>
> *Then said I, Lo, I come (in the volume of the book it is written of me,) to do thy will, O God* (Hebrews 10:5-7).

His supernatural entry into the world set the stage for a life of dominion.

At twelve years of age, Jesus showed amazing wisdom. He not only quizzed the shrewd lawyers in Jerusalem, but He answered their questions as well. The authority of His words and answers amazed the intellectuals of Jerusalem:

> *And it came to pass, that after three days they found him in the temple, sitting in the midst of the doctors, both hearing them, and asking them questions.*
>
> *And all that heard him were astonished at his understanding and answers* (Luke 2:46, 47).

Authority over Temptation

Immediately after Jesus was baptized by John, the Spirit of God descended upon Him, and the Father said, *This is my beloved Son, in whom I am well pleased* (Matthew 3:17). Jesus then went forth into the wilderness to exercise dominion over the temptations of the devil.

Jesus met temptations of the spirit, temptations of the soul, and physical temptations while living in a body of flesh. He defeated them all with the power of the written Word of God and the word of His testimony.

> *Jesus defeated temptations with the power of the written Word of God and the word of His testimony.*

It is written, He powerfully declared, *Man shall not live by bread alone, but by every word that proceedeth out of the mouth of God* (Matthew 4:4).

Dominion over Tradition

Jesus' teaching was not like any the people of His day had ever heard, and they recognized the difference immediately. What made His teaching different?

And it came to pass, when Jesus had ended these sayings, the people were astonished at his doctrine: For he taught them as one having authority, and not as the scribes (Matthew 7:28, 29).

The *authority* in His teaching made the difference.

The Spirit of might was upon Jesus, and everyone stood back and watched while He worked.

> *And Jesus went into the temple of God, and cast out all them that sold and bought in the temple, and overthrew the tables of the moneychangers, and the seats of them that sold doves,*
>
> *And said unto them, It is written, My house shall be called the house of prayer; but ye have made it a den of thieves.*
>
> *And the blind and the lame came to him in the temple; and he healed them.*
>
> *And when the chief priests and scribes saw the wonderful things that he did, and the children crying in the temple, and saying, Hosanna to the Son of David; they were sore displeased* (Matthew 21:12-15).

After Jesus loosed the temple of God from men's traditions, the blind and the lame came to him; and He healed them.

Tradition is a terrible destructive influence that can bury you. You can get so steeped in tradition that you say, "It's always been done that way, and we are always going to do it that way." If you are bound by tradition, God cannot move in your life in a new way to help and bless you.

If you are bound by tradition, God cannot move in your life in a new way to help and bless you.

Dominion Over Nature

At the beginning of Christ's public ministry, His first miracle turned spring water into sparkling, delicious wine (John 2:1-11). This was accomplished without the fermentation process of nature.

This beginning of miracles did Jesus in Cana of Galilee, and manifested forth his glory; and his disciples believed on him (John 2:11).

Those around Jesus were suddenly aware of His dominion as they observed nature obeying Him!

Christ showed Himself to be the master of nature by walking on the Sea of Galilee. His disciples were troubled and amazed at such dominion: *And in the fourth watch of the night Jesus went unto them, walking on the sea. And when the disciples saw him walking on the sea, they were troubled. . .* (Matthew 14: 25, 26).

Jesus further demonstrated His power over nature by calming the tempestuous sea with a spoken word:

> *And there arose a great storm of wind, and the waves beat into the ship, so that it was now full.*
>
> *And he was in the hinder part of the ship, asleep on a pillow: and they awake him, and say unto him, Master, carest thou not that we perish?*
>
> *And he arose, and rebuked the wind, and said unto the sea, Peace, be still. And the wind ceased, and there was a great calm.*
>
> *And he said unto them, Why are ye so fearful? How is it that ye have no faith?*

And they feared exceedingly, and said one to another, What manner of man is this, that even the wind and the sea obey him? (Mark 4:37-41).

God created the earth with a perfect weather system, but Satan brought about devastating upheaval. As a result, storms and winds have driven man—who was created to rule the world—to seek protection from the elements.

When Jesus rebuked the storm and spoke to the sea, they obeyed His words. Believers have that same dominion over the elements, and the Lord expects us to use our authority. In the ship Jesus rebuked His disciples for being fearful and faithless.

Dominion over Disease and Sickness

How God anointed Jesus of Nazareth with the Holy Ghost and with power: who went about doing good, and healing all that were oppressed of the devil; for God was with him (Acts 10:38).

Throughout His earthly walk, Jesus went about doing good and healing. He exercised complete dominion over the disease and sickness Satan had brought to mankind.

> *Throughout His earthly walk . . . Jesus exercised complete dominion over the disease and sickness Satan had brought to mankind.*

A Roman centurion—a man who understood authority—came to Jesus on behalf of his paralyzed servant who was sick at home. When Jesus said, "I will come and heal him," the centurion answered:

> *Lord, I am not worthy that thou shouldest come under my roof: but speak the word only, and my servant shall be healed.*
>
> *For I am a man under authority, having soldiers under me: and I say to this man, Go, and he goeth; and to another, Come, and he cometh; and to my servant, Do this, and he doeth it.*
>
> *When Jesus heard it, he marvelled, and said to them that followed, Verily I say unto you, I have not found so great faith, no, not in Israel. . . .*
>
> *And Jesus said unto the centurion, Go thy way; and as thou hast believed, so be it done unto thee. And his servant was healed in the selfsame hour* (Matthew 8:8-10, 13).

Christ healed that servant with the spoken word of authority. The Roman officer's faith drew a commendation from Jesus. By contrast, Jesus' disciples had not recognized His authority, and Jesus rebuked them for their lack of faith (Mark 4:40).

Many scriptures reveal that Jesus Christ always exercised authority over sickness and disease. He never failed to heal those brought to Him: *When the even was come, they brought unto him many that were possessed with devils: and he cast out the spirits with his word, and healed all that were sick* (Matthew 8:16).

The Lord Jesus never revealed any evidence of fear over the forces of nature or disease. He dominated them completely.

Dominion over Demons and Death

From the beginning of His ministry, the Lord Jesus demonstrated His *power over evil spirits* of all kinds.

> ### *Jesus demonstrated His power over evil spirits of all kinds.*

The following is only one of several recorded instances. In this passage demons recognized Jesus and feared Him. They raged against their victim in a final effort to remain, but the words of faith from Jesus caused them to leave and set the man free. People could see the authority and power of Jesus over the evil spirit.

> *And in the synagogue there was a man, which had a spirit of an unclean devil, and cried out with a loud voice,*
>
> *Saying, Let us alone: what have we to do with thee, thou Jesus of Nazareth? art thou come to destroy us? I know thee who thou art; the Holy One of God.*
>
> *And Jesus rebuked him, saying, Hold thy peace, and come out of him. And when the*

devil had thrown him in the midst, he came out of him, and hurt him not.

And they were all amazed, and spake among themselves, saying, What a word is this! for with authority and power he commandeth the unclean spirits and they came out (Luke 4:33-36).

The demoniac of Gadara had 2000 or more such demons. Mary Magdalene had seven. Some people had spirits of blindness, others had spirits of dumbness, and many had unclean spirits; but they all yielded to Christ's dominion.

Death had to yield to Christ's dominion, too. The Lord Jesus asserted His authority over the powers of death by raising the dead.

He raised a girl from the dead while she was still in her home (Mark 5).

He raised a boy from the dead as he lay on his funeral bier (Luke 7:11-15).

He raised Lazarus after he had been dead for four days (John 11).

Christ possessed dominion over death and over all the power of the enemy.

The Lord of Glory

The Apostle Paul called the demonic powers in the world system *princes of this world, that come to nought* (1 Corinthians 2:6).

Then he spoke of the glorious plan of God that brought them to nothing.

But we speak the wisdom of God in a mystery, even the hidden wisdom, which God ordained before the world unto our glory:

Which none of the princes of this world knew: for had they known it, they would not have crucified the Lord of glory (1 Corinthians 2:7, 8).

The devil and his cohorts played right into the plan of God and brought about their own doom when they crucified Jesus. In His death, burial, and resurrection, Jesus completely destroyed the power of the enemy and delivered mankind.

> ***In His death, burial, and resurrection, Jesus completely destroyed the power of the enemy.***

Forasmuch then as the children are partakers of flesh and blood, he also himself likewise took part of the same; that through death he might destroy him that had the power of death, that is, the devil;

And deliver them who through fear of death were all their lifetime subject to bondage (Hebrews 2:14, 15).

When Jesus appeared to John the Revelator on the Isle of Patmos, He said, *I am he that liveth, and was dead; and, behold, I am alive for evermore, Amen; and have the keys of hell and of death* (Revelation 1:18). Keys represent authority.

After His resurrection, Jesus remained with His followers for forty days. He concluded His earthly ministry by declaring, *All power is given unto me in heaven and in earth* (Matthew 28:18).

That is *supreme dominion!* But Jesus did not stop there. Because He was given all power, Jesus was able to add the command to go to all the nations, teaching and baptizing in the name of the Father, Son, and Holy Spirit (Matthew 28:19).

No person on record has revealed and taught dominion like the Lord Jesus. The Bible says of Him, *In whom are hid all the treasures of wisdom and knowledge* (Colossians 2:3).

Jesus delegated His authority on the earth to His Body, the Church.

> ### *Jesus delegated His authority on the earth to His Body, the Church.*

Mark's account of the momentous delegation of authority declares that Jesus said:

> *And these signs shall follow them that believe; In my name shall they cast out devils; they shall speak with new tongues;*
>
> *They shall take up serpents; and if they drink any deadly thing, it shall not hurt them; they shall lay hands on the sick, and they shall recover* (Mark 16:17, 18).

263

Dominion over demons, over disease, and over all the power of the devil was and is now restored to Christ's Body, the Church, *in His name!*

26
Exercising Collective Dominion

Satan not only tries to steal personal dominion and individual authority, but he works hard to enslave entire communities, cities, and nations. He does this through lying philosophies taught in secular schools, books, media, and even in some churches. Empires are destroyed through lies that lead to weakness.

Pagan religions enslave entire nations. From the highest to the lowest the people bow down in fear before idols and superstitions. These nations abound in fear, poverty, disease, and all that Satan brought with him into the earth.

But God offers collective dominion to those who will accept it!

Communities of Dominion

A community can exercise collective dominion if a strong spiritual leader is in control. Abraham's pilgrims became a large community. He had 318 armed servants who defeated and destroyed four kings and their armies. This battle was the first recorded conflict in the Bible.

How exciting it must have been to have lived in that community. General Abraham himself trained and equipped the army. He taught his men they could conquer in spite of great odds because they had added power—Jehovah God's power!

There are cities in the world where the saints of God have taken dominion over entire areas.

This was true in Zion, Illinois, for many years. It was formed as a Christian city, and for a long time no cigarettes or alcoholic beverages were permitted to be sold. People could sense the Spirit of the Lord as they entered the area.

So-called "evangelical cities" have a very different "feeling" than pagan cities. For example, I found Calcutta, India, with its millions of Hindu gods, to be one of the most depressing cities on the face of the earth. The city is named after Cali, a female goddess. Cali is a fierce devil. When you see her image at the great temple, her tongue sticks out about six inches wide and eight inches long. This goddess demands blood. Her followers bring goats to the temple and cut their throats, letting the blood flow into a groove under the hideous idol. Her devotees then splash their faces and drink the hot goat blood. I have been there several times, and it is sickening. The entire area reeks of Satan. Sin, sickness, poverty, and death reign. Anyone can see it and feel it.

On the other hand, there are several cities in the United States today that are especially possessed by God's people and His Spirit. Many great works of the Kingdom of God go forth from them. When you enter the city, the very atmosphere warms your whole being.

> *Several cities in the U.S. are especially possessed by God's people and His Spirit . . . the very atmosphere warms your whole being.*

I know a city affected by the dominion of the saints. One morning the pastor of a small church in that town walked by the corner bar on his way to the post office. He had been going by that bar for years. But that morning he placed his hand on the old brick wall and cursed the bar in the same manner his Master had done to a fig tree two thousand years before.

In a few weeks, the bar closed. Someone reopened it, but it closed again. The pastor had forgotten how he had prayed until the Spirit of the Lord reminded him.

A young woman, who was youth director of the church, was impressed by the Spirit to claim the bar for God's service. After much hard work, the former bar reopened as an evangelical outreach center for youth.

A few doors down the street was an old pool hall. The youth workers decided they needed the building for their ministry, so they began to pray. Within a few months, the pool hall went out of business and a recreation center for restless young people was opened in its place. This small town is being possessed by the people of God who are taking dominion over the works of Satan.

Jesus wept over Jerusalem, the largest city in Israel at that time. Today, we should weep over the great cities of our land lest they become throne rooms of the devil's power.

No power can stand before the living Church. The Lord Jesus promised that even the gates of hell could not stop His Church. Let's advance on the big cities. Let's possess our communities for Christ.

The City of God

Abraham looked for a city whose builder and maker is God (Hebrews 11:10). And so do we. *But ye are come unto mount Sion, and unto the city of the living God, the heavenly Jerusalem* (Hebrews 12:22).

God's Word paints a picture of a city where divine dominion reigns supreme. The only things missing are the curses and problems Satan brought with him when he usurped man's rule.

And I saw a new heaven and a new earth: for the first heaven and the first earth were passed away; and there was no more sea.

And I John saw the holy city, new Jerusalem, coming down from God out of heaven, prepared as a bride adorned for her husband.

And I heard a great voice out of heaven saying, Behold, the tabernacle of God is with men, and he will dwell with them, and they shall be his people, and God himself shall be with them, and be their God.

And God shall wipe away all tears from

their eyes; and there shall be no more death, neither sorrow, nor crying, neither shall there be any more pain: for the former things are passed away (Revelation 21:1-4).

God's glory fills the holy city. Every citizen of the heavenly city is a victor. Every person is a redeemed and immortal soul.

And he carried me away in the spirit to a great and high mountain, and shewed me that great city, the holy Jerusalem, descending out of heaven from God,
Having the glory of God. . . .
And I saw no temple therein: for the Lord God Almighty and the Lamb are the temple of it.
And the city had no need of the sun, neither of the moon, to shine in it: for the glory of God did lighten it, and the Lamb is the light thereof (Revelation 21:10, 11, 22, 23).

God's glory fills His temple in the earth today. We, the Church, are that living temple. When we take the dominion that is now ours, His glory enlightens the places we possess. For the Lamb is our light indeed.

> **When we take the dominion that is ours, God's glory enlightens the places we possess.**

Nations of Dominion

When Israel honored God, no enemy could stand against her. If they came before her one way, they fled before her seven ways. The Red Sea's waters rolled back to let the nation of Israel through. Jericho's walls tumbled before the people of Israel. Canaan's inhabitants were no match for Israel's God. The All-Sufficient One was her provider, and the Lord of Hosts was her healer.

The Most High God was Israel's strength and shield. It was His desire that everyone should look at her dominion over all the power of the enemy and say, "There is a God in Israel!" Then, like Rahab, they would want to know Him as their God.

But nations, like individuals, must decide to serve God. Israel's choices were set before her when God said, *I call heaven and earth to record this day against you, that I have set before you life and death, blessing and cursing: therefore choose life, that both thou and thy seed may live* (Deuteronomy 30:19).

Ancient Israel forsook her God to worship devils (Deuteronomy 32:17). When she did, she gave up her dominion. Her inhabitants were dispersed throughout the earth, leaving her land idle and desolate for hundreds of years.

The United States of America is one of the most unique nations of all times. Early settlers came to her shores seeking religious freedom. In-depth studies into Virginia's earliest visitors from Europe reveal startling facts of the leading of the Spirit of God.

We have been known to the world as a Christian

nation. "In God We Trust" is stamped on our money. "One nation, under God" is recited in our pledge of allegiance to the flag.

Even today the gospel goes forth from this nation as no other in history. The majority of all missionary work is supported from this nation by the sacrificial giving of millions of Christians.

Freedom to worship, freedom to assemble, freedom of speech, freedom of the press—all these are birthrights often unappreciated by those of us born within America's domain.

> *Freedom to worship, freedom to assemble, freedom of speech, freedom of the press—all these are birthrights often unappreciated by those of us born within America's domain.*

Our nation has blessed Israel and known the blessing that results according to God's Word (Genesis 12:3).

In 1956, however, America took a position against Israel. Our commanders demanded that France and Britain remove their troops from the Suez Canal Zone. Israel was forced to give back to Egypt the entire Sinai that Israeli soldiers had taken in battle. America cut off relations with Israel, and no planes were permitted to land and no ships could dock. My family and I lived in Jerusalem at that time, and it was France that fed us.

Since that time, America has lost ground and glory in Korea, Vietnam, Cuba, Africa, Asia, and South America.

God has placed the state of a nation into the hands of His people who dwell there:

> *If my people, which are called by my name, shall humble themselves, and pray, and seek my face, and turn from their wicked ways; then will I hear from heaven, and will forgive their sin, and will heal their land* (2 Chronicles 7:14).

The people of God living in a land can exercise their collective dominion. They can hold the reins of the nation in their hands.

Christians everywhere should practice the following New Testament admonition to pray for the leaders of their government:

> *I exhort therefore, that, first of all, supplications, prayers, intercessions, and giving of thanks, be made for all men;*
> *For kings, and for all that are in authority; that we may lead a quiet and peaceable life in all godliness and honesty.*
> *For this is good and acceptable in the sight of God our Saviour;*
> *Who will have all men to be saved, and to come unto the knowledge of the truth* (1 Timothy 2:1-4).

The Church in the United States is responsible before God for this nation. Let us rise up and take our dominion on behalf of our country—and on behalf of the countless millions of lost humanity whom God would have to be saved. The gospel must continue to go forth freely from the United States of America.

27
Power Against Power

Today's generation is a *power* generation. New power drugs, power weapons, and power machines are developed every year. We have power politics with men struggling for position. The world is drunk on power—*dominion.* Man loves power—from the popping of an inch-long firecracker to the blasting of an atomic bomb. The whole world is seeking greater power.

We dig for the hidden power of coal that has lain dormant for centuries. It is transformed into power to move engines and heat furnaces.

We drive machinery deep into the bowels of the earth to suck out oil and gas for our mechanized age. Our society is dependent on electric power. Without it cities are paralyzed and modern conveniences are obsolete.

When man took hold of atomic power to harness and release it, two cities in Japan were disintegrated. Since that day, the world has lived in fear of a nuclear holocaust.

In the air above us, radio waves speed around the world at 180,000 miles per second. That's seven times around the world in one second!

At our television station here in South Bend,

Indiana, we have a link-up with a satellite. A television broadcast image can leave Virginia or North Carolina or California—or any other place producing an up-link—and travel 22,300 miles above the earth to the satellite and back down through the down-link in South Bend in less than a second. You can barely bat your eye before it is up and back down again.

Our world is power conscious, but power can be used in two ways—constructively or destructively. Man has to decide which way to use power.

The Power of Sin

The most destructive force in the universe is sin. It is the greatest destroyer of mankind.

Organized crime, an evil that has hurt many people, operates through the power of sin. Newscasts are replete with reports of murders in small hamlets and large cities—men killing men, women killing women, children killing children. Mankind seems to have lost respect for human life and human dignity.

Sin causes all murder, thefts, and adultery. Drunkenness, gambling, and cheating are the result of sin. All moral uncleanness comes from sin. Sin has power.

No human can tackle the power of sin and win over it. Your human power cannot stand up against sin's power because the devil is the originator of sin. He is the head captain of everyone who steals, kills, or destroys. *The thief cometh not, but for to steal, and to kill, and to destroy. . .* (John 10:10). Natural human strength is no match for Satan's power.

The Bible describes Satan in his original state. In

heaven he was *full of wisdom, and perfect in beauty* (Ezekiel 28:12). He was adorned with every perfect stone that glitters—diamonds, rubies, and other precious stones (Ezekiel 28:13).

But Lucifer turned his God-given will against God. Instead of choosing to worship God, he rebelled against his Creator and fell from his place of beauty and glory. Isaiah 14:12-15 tells the terrible story. Jesus told His disciples how He had beheld Satan as lightning fall from heaven (Luke 10:18).

Isaiah 14:12 identifies him as the one who weakened the nations. Any nation weakened by Satan's power is eventually destroyed. Lucifer is described as the one who *made the earth to tremble* (Isaiah 14:16). Every time there is war, revolution, or turmoil, the devil is the force behind it. He "shakes kingdoms" and creates havoc throughout the world (Isaiah 14:16).

A few days after World War II was over, I went to Europe. In London I saw the buildings where I had lived completely destroyed. The Bible college where I had taught was gone. In France whole cities where I had preached many times were nothing but rubble. I just stood there and cried, "Oh, God! Oh, God!"

Any time you see destruction, there is a sinister personality close by—the devil. His ministry is one of destruction.

The Power of Our Savior

God's Word tells us of a far greater power than Satan. *But we preach Christ crucified, unto the Jews a stumblingblock, and unto the Greeks foolishness; but unto them which are called, both Jews and Greeks, Christ the power of God, and the wisdom of God* (1 Corinthians 1:23, 24).

What is Christ? Christ is the power of God! *For I am not ashamed of the gospel of Christ: for it is the power of God unto salvation to everyone that believeth . . .* (Romans 1:16).

The gospel is the power of God. The gospel we preach is not words, not notions, not philosophic ideas— it is the power of God! *But as many as received him, to them gave he power to become the sons of God, even to them that believe on his name* (John 1:12).

> **The gospel we preach is not words, not notions, not philosophic ideas— it is the power of God!**

When we receive Christ into our hearts, something happens to us. To as many as receive Him, He gives power.

But ye shall receive power, after that the Holy Ghost is come upon you: and ye shall be witnesses unto me both in Jerusalem, and in all Judaea, and in Samaria, and unto the uttermost part of the earth (Acts 1:8).

We receive power after the Holy Spirit comes upon us. Aren't you glad for that?

When I think of power against power, it reminds

me of a dam. To stop a river from running, you dam it up and make a lake out of it. Which is stronger—the water flowing down the river or the dam? If the dam has been properly engineered, it can stand against the force of the water. Flood waters rise against it, but the dam remains firmly in place. Its staying power is stronger than the moving power—so the moving power can do nothing but back off.

When it is power against power, the weaker power must back off. When it is power against power, one power will always supersede.

God's power will always supersede the power of evil when we exercise it. God wants to bring His children to the place where we know and exercise our God-given power.

> *God's power will always supersede the power of evil when we exercise it.*

When Satan comes against God's people, he should find a dam of faith holding him back. We should say, "Back off, waters of evil, we're here to stay. We're here to hold you back and to tell you how far you can go."

Steel can be made so tough that steel won't cut steel. But a little diamond put into a vice can cut through the strongest piece of steel. Why? It's force against force—power against power. Something has to give.

The steel says, "I am tough."

The diamond says, "Yes, but I am tougher. You yield to me. I am the boss."

Jesus was talking about power against power when He said,

> *But if I cast out devils by the Spirit of God, then the kingdom of God is come unto you.*
>
> *Or else how can one enter into a strong man's house, and spoil his goods, except he first bind the strong man? and then he will spoil his house* (Matthew 12:28, 29).

The devil may be tough, but we are tougher. He may be strong, but we are stronger. We have to know this principle, however, before it will be effective in our lives. We must live with the power and divine authority of God.

In Indonesia some years ago I met a little Dutch missionary from Holland. When she first went back into the mountains of Indonesia to preach the gospel, the local witch doctor told her to leave. He said she was in his territory.

This little missionary said, "You don't have any territory. I am going to stay."

He said, "No! I don't like other witch doctors coming in here. I respect other witch doctors. I don't go into their places, and I don't want them in mine."

She said, "I'm no witch doctor."

He said, "You act like one."

They quarreled for some time. Finally, the witch

doctor said, "Let's see who has the most power. The one who has less power, let that one leave."

The missionary agreed.

The witch doctor said, "Let's meet on a certain day and ask everybody to come."

On that day, the whole village came to see what was going to happen. They thought two witch doctors were going to have a contest to decide who would be boss of that community.

The young woman missionary and the witch doctor stepped onto a platform.

The witch doctor looked at her and said, "Do something."

She didn't know what to do, so she said, "You do something."

He lay down on the floor before all the people and became stiff as a board. Very slowly, the powers of levitation caught him, and he rose up ankle high, then knee high, until he floated in the air.

The people were amazed. Surely he was the most powerful, they said.

The Dutch girl thought, *I know I can't float. I guess I'll have to leave.*

God said, "No, you don't!"

She said, "Well, what am I going to do?"

God said, "Get him down! Put your foot on his belly and push him over."

So she walked over to him, pulled up her long skirt a little, put her foot on his belly, and pushed him against the floor.

Then God said, "Cast the devil out of him!"

So she said, "Come out of him in the name of Jesus!"

The devil came out at her command. When the man came to his senses, he didn't know where he was. He had been so possessed by the devil that he hadn't been in his right mind. He didn't even know the contest was taking place.

He said, "Where am I? What am I doing here? What is this all about?"

She reached over and pulled him up to a sitting position. She told him what had happened, and he received Jesus as his Savior. She laid hands on him, and he received the Holy Spirit.

As a result, the missionary was made the administrator of the town, and the former witch doctor became the mayor. When they had a community meeting, she sat in a chair beside him, giving advice only when she felt he needed help. Soon the village became known as the Refugee Town. Anyone who had received Jesus and was being persecuted could come there and live with them.

In our everyday lives, we face problems and situations that are power against power. It is up to us to decide who is the winner.

Jesus Christ is the winner, and God wants each of us to be winners, too. He has made it possible for us always to triumph in Christ Jesus. God wants every one of us to know and confess His mighty power. You cannot confess defeat and at the same time give Jesus authority in your life. You must confess victory in Jesus' name.

Until the end of this age, it will be power against power. But God's Word has settled forever the fact that the greater power resides in the believer—not in the world.

> ### *The greater power resides in the believer—not in the world.*

Ye are of God, little children, and have overcome them: because greater is he that is in you, than he that is in the world (1 John 4:4).

The "them" we "have overcome" are demons and evil spirits. The Greater One Who is in us is Jesus through the power of the Holy Spirit. The devil is *he that is in the world.*

Jesus is the Greater One. He is in you. You are not a loser. You are a winner. So take your place of dominion—it's yours!

28
Winning the Prize

All new model automobiles are tested to see if they can perform efficiently when the rubber meets the road. Your life is the same. When the rubber meets the road, what kind of a person are you? Are you a quitter? Are you a grumbler? Or are you an endurer?

James 1:12 says, *Blessed is the man that endureth temptation: for when he is tried, he shall receive the crown of life, which the Lord hath promised to them that love him.*

The word "blessed" is related to joy. We could say, "Joyful is the man who endures temptation." The joy comes on the other end—not so much in the midst of the temptation. Joy results from enduring. The trying or the testing reveals your true character.

How to Resist Temptation

Resisting temptation is like any other aspect of the Christian life—certain principles must be followed in order for you to be successful at it. If you put these guidelines into practice, you will have victory over temptation.

First, set your heart. Your heart must be set against the source of your temptation. If you think one way one day and another way the next, then you are not stable (James 1:8). Any time you don't know what is right, you're going to do the wrong thing.

Daniel purposed in his heart that he would not defile himself with the portion of the king's meat (Daniel 1:8). Daniel knew what was right, and he said, "I purpose in my heart I will not defile myself." How could the best food in the world be defiled? In Babylon all the meat was offered up to idols before it was eaten. Daniel would have been worshipping the devil if he had eaten it. He purposed in his heart, he stood his ground, and God honored him for it.

Second, be careful who you listen to. Other people may try to influence you to be unfaithful to God.

Job's wife said to him, *Dost thou still retain thine integrity?* (Job 2:9). Someone today might ask, "Do you still go to church after all that has happened to you?"

Job's wife also suggested that he *curse God and die,* but Job responded to her in the right way. "You're talking like a foolish woman!" he replied.

Listening to wrong counsel can get you into trouble and cause you to sin. But Job refused to take his wife's advice. The Bible says, *In all this did not Job sin with his lips* (v. 10). Get your direction from God and avoid the counsel of the ungodly.

> ### *Get your direction from God and avoid the counsel of the ungodly.*

Third, refuse to have companionship with worldly people. Ungodly companions can turn your heart away from God and His ways.

Proverbs 4:14 says, *Enter not into the path of the wicked and go not in the way of evil men.*

If your companions are wicked people, then you're going to become like them. If you like to be with your old cronies, you are going to fall back into your old ways.

If you want to live in glory and victory, you must choose godly companions. In order to walk with God, you must walk with God's people.

Fourth, be prepared to face temptation. If you're going to be victorious in your Christian living, you need to be prepared spiritually.

Ephesians 6:13 says, *Take unto you the whole armour of God, that ye may be able to withstand in the evil day, and having done all, to stand. Stand therefore. . . .* When you have done everything, keep on standing.

Why Bother to Resist?

Why should we shun evil and resist temptation? Because Christ commands us to live in a state of perfection. We may not be able to live in ultimate perfection, but we can experience perfection of love and an attitude of duty toward God. Jesus said, *Be ye therefore perfect, even as your Father which is in heaven is perfect* (Matthew 5:48).

If you're going to live a victorious life, don't move toward degradation—move toward perfection. Be a better person today than you were yesterday. Be more mature in your Christian walk this week than you were last week.

> *If you're going to live a victorious life,*
> *don't move toward degradation—*
> *move toward perfection.*

The Apostle Paul said, *I keep under my body, and bring it into subjection: lest that by any means, when I have preached to others, I myself should be a castaway* (1 Corinthians 9:27).

Plenty of people can tell you how to live right yet not do it themselves. Every sinner in town can give you a one-hour sermon on how to live right while he goes on swearing, committing adultery, and getting drunk.

Paul says, "If I don't keep my body under control and bring it under subjection, then when I have talked to others, I myself will be a castaway. I must not only talk to you, but I must live it myself."

Two ministers telephoned and asked me to pray for them. Although they both have large churches and successful ministries, these pastors were depressed. How can they minister joy to their people if they are in a state of depression?

Don't instruct others, and then become a castaway. You have to shun temptation in Jesus' name.

Avoiding Mistakes

The Apostle Paul said, *All these things happened unto them for ensamples: and they are written for our admonition. . .* (1 Corinthians 10:11). If you see what's happened to others by their transgressions, that will keep you from falling. The things that happened to people throughout the Old Testament were written for our admonition.

Mr. Howard Carter, my teacher and mentor, said, "Don't ever think of beginning where I did. I've been there; you begin where I quit. You begin here and then go on." He would rebuke me sometimes and say, "I've seen young men who had great privileges but who never amounted to anything. What are you going to do?"

"I'm going to do my best," I'd say.

"You better do more than that!" was his reply. For years he prodded me into believing for God's best.

When we see the shipwreck of others, we don't have to take the same boat. When we see the discouragement of others, we don't have to jump in that pool of despondency. When we see others stumbling along the pathway of life, we don't have to take that same road. There is a way of victory for everyone of us.

> ***When we see the shipwreck of others, we don't have to take the same boat.***

When you read about the sins of Samson and David, you can avoid making the same mistakes. Their trials and temptations are written in the Bible so you won't fall into the same traps.

James 4:7 shows us the strength and dominion we have over sin. James says, *Submit yourselves therefore to God. Resist the devil, and he will flee from you.* Many of us know the last part of the verse, but we leave off the conditional part.

First, submit yourself to God by surrendering your life completely to Him. After you have done that, then you have a right to tell the devil to leave. When you've submitted to God and you command Satan to leave, he has to go.

If you're not submitted to God, the devil does not have to obey you. If you're living in sin, you can't say, "Get away from me, devil!" He won't pay attention to you. He'll just hug you a little tighter! But if you're living under God's discipline, the devil cannot touch you.

> *If you're living under God's discipline, the devil cannot touch you.*

Running to Win

How do we become strong in the Lord and in the power of His might? First Corinthians 9:24 says, *Know ye not that they which run in a race run all, but one receiveth the prize? So run, that ye may obtain.* We are victors when we put our energy into positive action.

This verse does not say if you sit in a rocking chair and rock along, you'll win a prize. It does not say if you sit in your lazyboy and watch television, you will receive a crown. The Bible says, "Run!" If we are going to be mighty men and women of God, we need to get into a spiritual training program. Those who run receive the prize, so don't quit.

Paul must have attended the Olympic Games when he visited Athens. He saw the young men—powerful, strong, and determined—training for the Olympics. As he watched them, Paul knew that any of those athletes who were striving for mastery or perfection were temperate in their lifestyle. *Every man that striveth for the mastery is temperate in all things* (1 Corinthians 9:25).

Athletes in training don't stay up late at night or gorge themselves on junk food. Anyone who strives for the mastery is temperate in all areas of life. If you are seeking to be a master, God says you must be temperate. A disciplined life is the key to victory.

Let us lay aside every weight, and the sin which doth so easily beset us, and let us run with patience the race that is set before us (Hebrews 12:1).

This is the secret to being a winner. Lay aside every sin that is weighing you down and keeping you from running the race to victory.

The rewards of a victorious life are worth all the effort you put into running the race. The man who endures temptation will receive *the crown of life* (James 1:12). The trial of your faith is *more precious than gold* (1 Peter 1:7).

Jesus says, *To him that overcometh will I grant to sit with me in my throne, even as I also overcame, and am set down with my Father in his throne* (Revelation 3:21).

When temptation comes, kick it out of the way and march forward. Live for Jesus and love God. If you truly love God and are committed to Him, you will be promoted by the Father to a higher grade in His Kingdom.

> ***If you truly love God and are committed to Him, you will be promoted by the Father to a higher grade in His Kingdom.***

In this life, we receive earthly rewards for the good we do. But we also live for the reward in heaven that will be given to all who have received eternal life. Do not let the devil discourage you. If he can get you to stay home from church, if he can get you to stop witnessing, if he can get you to stop praying, if he can get you to stop reading the Bible, he's the winner and you are the loser.

Pray this prayer with me:

> *Father, thank You for victorious living. The devil is defeated and destroyed. I am a winner on the side of Jesus, and I will be victorious. Anoint me in faith and courage to endure to the end and win the crown of life, in Jesus' name. Amen.*

Dominion over Satan and the world has been given to you, so take it—it's yours! *This is the victory that overcometh the world, **even our faith*** (1 John 5:4).

Dr. Lester Sumrall
1913-1996

The voice of Dr. Lester Sumrall remains prominent in the Christian world today. More than 65 years of ministry in over 100 nations made Dr. Sumrall a respected source of wisdom and understanding. He was an author, teacher, missionary, evangelist, and the pastor and founder of Christian Center Church in South Bend, Indiana. Throughout his lifetime, Dr. Sumrall worked tirelessly to fulfill The Great Commission by carrying the gospel to the ends of the earth. In 1957 he founded LeSEA, a multi-faceted global outreach. Today LeSEA's outreaches blanket the world through television, satellite, FM and short-wave radio, and LeSEA Global Feed the Hungry®. Would you like to be a part of feeding the spirit, soul, and body of the hungry? Call today! 1-888-TEAM-FTH (1-888-832-6384).

Prayerline:
(574) 291-1010

www.lesea.com

A Prayer of Salvation

If Jesus should come today, would you be ready? If you say the following prayer from the depths of your heart and surrender to Him as the Lord of your life, He will come in and instantly forgive you of all your sins. As you trust Him, you will be filled with hope and peace that only Jesus can offer.

If you are ready to make this commitment, please pray the following prayer out loud:

> *Dear Lord Jesus, I am a sinner. I do believe that you died and rose from the dead to save me from my sins. I want to be with you in heaven forever. Please forgive me of all my sins that I have committed. I here and now open my heart to You and ask You to come into my heart as Lord of my life and to be my personal Savior. Baptize me in your Spirit. Amen.*

Now that you have given your life to Christ, it is important to pray and read the Bible on a daily basis. It also is important to attend a Bible-believing church regularly. Doing these things will help you to walk in continual fellowship with the Lord.

We would be happy to rejoice with you, please feel free to write us at:

Christian Center Church
530 E. Ireland Rd.
South Bend, IN 46614

You may also call us at:
574-291-3292 (ask for the pastoral staff)

Other books by Dr. Lester Sumrall

Adventuring with Christ
Alien Entities
Angels to Help You
Be Bold and Walk Tall
Demons: The Answer Book
Exorcism
The Gifts and Ministries of the Holy Spirit
God's Blueprint for a Happy Home
The Human Face of Jesus
Jerusalem: Where Empires Die
Jihad—The Holy War
The Life Story of Lester Sumrall
Making of a Champion
Mercy: Man's Greatest Hope
The Militant Church
Mystery of Death
Panorama of Prophecy
Pioneers of Faith
Secrets of Answered Prayer
Supernatural Principalities & Powers
You Can Destroy the Gates of Hell
101 Questions & Answers on Demon Power

To receive a catalog of available
materials, contact:

LeSEA Publishing
530 E. Ireland Rd., South Bend, IN 46614
1-888-584-4847
www.leseapublishing.com